The Social Basis of the Rational Citizen

The Social Basis of the Rational Citizen

How Political Communication in Social Networks Improves Civic Competence

Sean Richey

LEXINGTON BOOKS
Lanham • Boulder • New York • Toronto • Plymouth, UK

Published by Lexington Books
A wholly owned subsidiary of Rowman & Littlefield
4501 Forbes Boulevard, Suite 200, Lanham, Maryland 20706
www.rowman.com

10 Thornbury Road, Plymouth PL6 7PP, United Kingdom

British Library Cataloguing in Publication Information Available

Library of Congress Cataloging-in-Publication Data
Richey, Sean.
   The social basis of the rational citizen : how political communication in social networks
improves civic competence / Sean Richey.
      pages cm
   Includes bibliographical references and index.
   ISBN 978-0-7391-6630-7 (cloth : alk. paper) -- ISBN 978-0-7391-8857-6 (electronic)
   1. Communication in politics. 2. Social networks--Political aspects. 3. Social media--
Political aspects. I. Title.
   JA85.R54 2014
   320.01'4--dc23
                                    2013032399
ISBN: 978-0-7391-6631-4 (pbk : alk, paper)

Printed in the United States of America

Contents

Chapter 1
Introduction

The paradox of mass democracy is: why are democracies so successful, when the public that controls the system is so apathetic and ignorant? We know that the public is often baffled when it comes to politics and manipulation by elites is a powerful force (Bartels 2005). If people are so easily swayed, why does democracy succeed? Elite theories are common explanations of how the system can survive with an irrational public. The theory states, generally, that it does not matter how much average citizens know about politics, if the people are not truly in control (Strauss 1964). As long as the elites that run the nation are knowledgeable and in control, we can trust that they will choose wisely. This theory tries to answer the paradox of mass democracy by simply denying the democratic nature of modern societies, which they imply is controlled by a technocratic elite.

This theory has a serious flaw, however, because elites are not much better at decision-making than the common people. For example, Tetlock (2005) shows that elites are rarely so advanced that they make optimal choices, and they are often blinded by ideology. Leaders also commonly make sub-optimal choices for predictable psychological reasons (Jervis 1993). Examples of quagmires that elite decision-making has created are all too common. In sum, elites are not so superior, and are often irrational. Thus, the paradox is not solved by elite theory, and we need to investigate how the system succeeds when decisions are made by dysfunctional citizens.

If elites are not able to provide enough guidance to explain democracy's success, then we must explain how citizens manage the system when they are so easily manipulated and confused. They do not know so much about poli-

1

tics and have major cognitive limitations that would make it unrealistic to make a rational choice by appropriately weighting and then selecting the optimal outcome (Lau and Redlawsk 2006). Two prominent theories examine macro-level political behavior and micro-level individual cognition to explain this paradox. At the macro level, Page and Shapiro (1992) suggest that irrational votes cancel each other out in a large electorate, leaving the outcome explained by rational voters. At the micro level, Popkin (1991) suggests that individuals use heuristics to take a shortcut in deciding who to vote for. This theory suggests that low-information voters will be able to discern enough information to make a good guess at which candidate is best for them by using heuristics.

While interesting and plausible, both theories ignore the powerful role of social networks in helping citizens make better choices. Taber (2003) argues for a compositional aggregation theory to explain the paradox. Here, democracy's success is explained by a complex system that aggregates preferences that are developed in small groups, with input from elites and mass media. This can achieve a preferable outcome if deliberation and discussion help the group decide. Social networks offer a potential solution to this paradox, but much more work is needed on whether social networking promotes rationality and how. The aim of this book is to empirically test the influence of the level between micro and macro, the level of interpersonal communication, in explaining why deciding together is better than deciding alone.

Social Network Influence

Social networking fascinates scholars, pundits and a billion Facebook users. Research shows that who we know has a vast impact on our political beliefs, actions and abilities. Networks are crucial to explain everything from how bills get through Congress, why people vote, how NGOs become successful in developing nations, and much more. Yet much of this literature is dispersed across many subfields, making it difficult to conceptualize. Further, despite having a long history in social science, research into political networks has exploded in the last fifteen years (Zuckerman 2005), with many novel findings which are not included in textbooks that mention social influence. These new studies have proliferated to a large extent and across many sub-fields in political science. Yet an in-depth analysis of the social basis of the rational voter is missing. To fill this void, this book provides a straightforward analysis of the most important hypothesized effect of social network influence on politics, social cognition.

Social networking in politics lies at the heart of a number of fascinating political questions and social concerns, including citizen competence, social movements, and voter mobilization. In response, scholarly interest in social networks has been growing. In fact, the American Political Science Association in 2010 started a new Political Networks section in response to demand for it from scholars.

Let's quickly summarize the main findings on how social networks improve political decision-making. At the micro level, scholars have examined group influence from the micro to the macro, by studying individual-level close-tie discussion networks, formal small-group membership, and networking between large groups. Early on, they addressed political socialization in childhood as the earliest form of social influence, which has been shown to have pervasive long-term impact on political attitudes and behavior. They also found a massive influence from membership in voluntary associations and social capital more generally on political behavior. Exciting new literatures have been developed on peer influence on everything from health to vote choices, with an important subset focusing on political discussion in heterogeneous and homogenous groups.

Turning to the macro level, scholars show how parties use social networks as a mobilization tool to get out the vote. They explain that interest groups are best conceived of as issue networks and how understanding social movements as social networks is beneficial. They describe how the laws of states mimic each other through a network-based process called diffusion. In research on congressional legislative networks, scholars show that getting bills passed in Congress depends crucially on who a congressperson is networked with. Presidential power is best understood as a power to establish a network of surrogates who extend the president's constitutionally limited powers. Research also shows that from panel effects in district and appellate courts to understanding jury decision-making, networks define the legal system. And finally, research shows that globalization has created the rise of transnational networks of NGOs that have to be connected both locally and globally to succeed. In sum, a review of the literature shows how crucial networks are to politics at all levels. Due to its importance to deliberative democratic theory, I will add to this literature by specifically focusing on rational decision-making through networking, also known as social cognition.

For research related to the theme of this book, social cognition, there have been several books that use a quantitative approach such as Huckfeldt, Johnson, and Sprague (2005), Huckfeldt and Sprague (1995), Mutz (2006) and Zuckerman (2005). These works offer substantial qualitative as well as quantitative analyses on political discussion and interpersonal communication and decision-making. But due to the large interest in decision-making in social networks, this research fills in a necessary part of the literature.

Theories of Network Influence

Recently, there has been a large growth in research on the influence of social networks in political science (Zuckerman 2005). Many recent studies focus on the impact of political discussion in informal social networks (e.g., Conover, Searing, and Crewe 2002; Huckfeldt, Mendez, and Osborn 2004; Mutz 2002). These studies find that most people do not deliberate, which is usually defined as formal public debates. Instead, they more often have informal political discussion with friends, family, and neighbors (Walsh 2004). Political discussions have many of the positive benefits that theorists assign to formal interpersonal communication (Bennett, Flickinger, and Rhine 2000). For example, political opinion quality increases when people discuss politics (Price and Capella 1999). Also, discussants are more likely to vote (Linimon and Joslyn 2002), and have more incentive to join political movements (McAdam and Paulsen 1993). For example, Brown and Brown (2003) show that political discussion among black church members promotes volunteering and electoral and non-electoral political participation.

This is not to say that political discussions are perfect exchanges of unbiased information among equals. Far from it; political discussions are often rife with biased information and imperceptions. But, Ikeda and Huckfeldt (2001) find that people are generally aware of which political party the people they discuss politics with support. Huckfeldt, Johnson, and Sprague (2004) find that many people have contentious disagreements within informal political discussions, which signifies that these are free exchanges of potential informative ideas. Importantly, Beck, Dalton, Greene, and Huckfeldt (2002) show that social networks promote vote similarity. In particular, persuasion among network members is a powerful influence on vote similarity (see Mutz, Sniderman, and Brody 1996). Cooke (2000) posits that there are five effects of political discussion (educative, communicative, procedural, egalitarian, and contextual), and all help citizens with democracy despite being an inherently flawed process. This literature provides clear evidence of the power of social networks.

This literature outlines three main theories of network influence. First, there are theories of group conformity. Zuckerman (2005) describes this as the dominant theory, and proponents stretch from Aristotle to Berelson, Lazarsfeld, and McPhee (1954). Simply put, pressure from cognitive dissonance and the desire to conform pushes people to associative mating. Thus, Republicans are more likely to associate with Republicans (and just happen to be around them), and also more likely to take a conservative friend's advice. This theory means that we take advice more readily from our close intimates. Huckfeldt, Johnson, and Sprague (2004) recently challenge this dominant view with an autoregressive theory. This theory states that influence is not based solely on conformity pressures with the discussant, but also is considered in relation to the other people the respondent discusses politics with, many of whom may hold opposing viewpoints. They show that most networks actually have some disagreement, often more than conformity. They state that this signifies that the influence of one person must be checked against the influence of the others in a network. Third, the opinion leader theory states that there is a necessary division of labor about knowledge and that people take advice from their knowledgeable associates (Neuman 1986). I will use lab experiments and survey data to test these theories on how they predict rational decision-making.

In addition to these social network theories, a broader but crucial theory is social capital. A crucial concept in modern social science is of the power of social capital to influence behavior (Putnam 2000). Social capital theorists include face-to-face discussion as one of its constituent parts. Social capital is defined as social networks, trust and reciprocity, civic engagement, and community involvement that facilitate collective action for mutual benefit (Coleman 1990; Putnam 1993). Social capital creates trust in one's community through shared experiences and social activities, which includes political discussion. For political scientists, the book that widely publicized the importance of social capital is Robert Putnam's work on local politics in contemporary Italy (Putnam 1993).

Putnam shows, first, that social interaction improves social skills that are a precondition of participation. For example, voluntary associations lead participants to encounter disagreement and conflict, engage in collective problem solving, and improve their social skills and leadership competence (Putnam 1993, 183). The positive impact of having in-depth discussions, coordinating voluntary organizations, and cultivating one's management capacity can be pervasive and be applicable to many contexts (Putnam 1993, 167). Human social interaction is a school of democracy, teaching the skills needed for political participation (Putnam 1993, 89-90). Note that in the theory, this skill development happens whether the goal of the interaction is recreational or overtly political.

Putnam's second point is that social networks—either formally in associations or formally in daily life—nourish trust and an understanding of the nation (Putnam 2000, 136). Research clearly shows that interpersonal communication has a profound influence on political behavior (Ryan 2010; Eveland, 2004; Gastil and Dillard 1999; Klofstad 2007, McClurg 2006; Huckfeldt 2001). The larger the network an individual has, the more frequent the exposure to heterogeneous others during economical dealings or social negotiations, and the greater the chance to access a wide variety of social resources. Both of these things enhance competence when dealing with dynamic societal change and give greater opportunity to learn about important issues in society. These factors, Putnam argued, initiate political participation, resulting in more affluent and productive communities. All of this leads us to believe that social networking will improve decision-making.

Social Networks and Rationality

Social networks are commonly shown to have a beneficial impact on political behavior (Beck, Dalton, Greene, and Huckfeldt 2002, Zuckerman 2005). For example, we know that more discussion and having knowledgeable discussants increases political knowledge. What we do not know is whether this also improves the quality of choice. Lau and Redlawsk (2006) show that campaigns influence correct voting, and that rationality can be manipulated. As part of a control variable on political sophistication, they include a measure of political discussion. This measure, commonly used, simply asks how many discussions about politics the respondent has had recently. Current literature on social networks shows that this question does not contain enough nuances to enable a test of the key questions here (see Huckfeldt and Sprague 1995). Further, they combine it with several other measures in an additive scale, so that the specific influence of discussion is unknown.

One commonly found effect is for people to learn from political discussion with opinion leaders (Huckfeldt 2001). This effect has been shown using large national sample surveys (e.g., Bennett, Fishfinger, and Rhine 2000) and experimental research (e.g., Mutz 2006). It matches a large literature from marketing that shows that word-of-mouth is a key determinant in the diffusion of innovations (Coleman, Katz, and Menzel 1957, Cox 1963, Herr, Kardes, and Kim 1991, Lau and Ng 2001, and Rogers 1962). People take recommendations seriously, and discussion is generally educative (Brown and Reingen 1987). The two-step hypothesis suggests that people can learn from each other in an easy division of labor, where someone knowledgeable about politics is able to improve the entire group's understanding. Interestingly, we can show through formal models that a relatively small number of knowledgeable people can inform a large number of citizens, and the process can achieve optimality without much initial knowledge by spreading knowledge through political discussion (Grofman, Owen, and Feld 1983).

But knowledge does not imply rationality. Knowledge is only one component of information processing. Whether political discussion can help people choose wisely is a different question than whether it educates them, because choice is bounded by cognitive limitations that are greater than simply a lack of knowledge. Social psychology shows that even when all information needed to make an optimal decision is present, people still choose poorly (e.g., see Tversky and Kahneman 1979). To choose rationally, citizens would have to be able to apply the increased knowledge from discussion to a greater, more abstract understanding of complex causal relationships and the opposing arguments of the political world. Thus, we need to investigate whether political discussion can help overcome cognitive limitations as well as a lack of political knowledge.

It is often suggested that exposure to multiple sources of information improves not only knowledge, but also decision-making (Lazarsfeld, Berelson, and Gaudet 1944). Combining diverse bits of opinions and information in a conversation, which may overlap with other conversations, may equal a sum greater than its parts. Page (2008) shows that when leaders decide alone they are far more prone to error than group decision-making. More often group decision-making leads to superior outcomes, because one person's mistakes are corrected by the group.

This is particularly true when there are multiple, perhaps opposing, viewpoints in the group. Druckman (2004) shows that the irrational framing effects found by Tversky and Kahneman—which are often pointed to by critics of democracy—are not present when allowing people to discuss their choices. This suggests that discussion promotes rational choices. In this book, I show through laboratory experiments and survey research that discussion improves rational decision-making, and this helps us understand how mass democracy can be successful.

Institutional Influences on Political Discussion

Once I establish that rationality benefits from discussion, the next question should be what promotes discussion. Thus, I also want to examine the context which sponsors or limits discussion. The nature of institutional influence on social networking is debated frequently in the literature. Miller and Jackman (1998) describe an internal inconsistency within social network scholarship as to whether social networking is endogenous or exogenous of institutions. One perspective is that societal structures and institutions create environments that foster communicative life-spheres where everyday deliberation flourishes. Thus, social networking is endogenous to institutions. The alternative exogenous view is that social capital is present in the form of political culture, and it is what influences institutional performance. Miller and Jackman (1998) find that these ideas are inconsistent and cannot be merged into a workable research agenda. They prefer the endogenous approach due to a series of common methodological concerns with the exogenous approach

The social network literature has been criticized for being "oblivious to institutions and structural causation" (Edwards and Foley 2001, 229). For example, a debated question was whether governmental reforms can create more social capital. Putnam (1993, 1995, and 2001) presents evidence that areas with higher levels of social capital have more responsive and efficient democracies. Skocpol critiques Putnam by arguing that without state structures to permit the existence of these groups, encourage their activities, and listen to their voices, social capital will not be effective (Skocpol and Ganz 2000). Putnam (1993) argues that social capital evolves from independently organized volunteer groups; thus, these groups affect government from the "bottom up." Skocpol and Ganz 2000 disagree and say that institutional structures are the source of social capital. The institutional structure determines whether these volunteer groups are present and effective; thus, social capital evolves "top down." Skocpol brings the state back into social capital research by examining historic evidence of civic associations and their relationship with the federal government (Skocpol and Ganz 2000).

One way to get at this question is to examine changes in institutions to see if they alter networking after the change. I take this approach below, by examining the simulative effect of campaigns and the design of electoral institutions. Specifically, I look at Oregon's vote by-mail reform and the influence of campaign spending. I show that campaign spending increases both political discussion and also political advocacy. This shows that engaged campaigns that seek to mobilize voters also spark down-the-line political communication in interpersonal settings. Potential reforms to make electoral campaigns more competitive (which should feature more spending) should also consider that the increased discussion and advocacy associated with these competitive campaigns will also lead to better decision-making.

In Oregon, I examine what else was affected by this change in electoral system, aside from the impact on voter turnout—which was the goal of the reform. I ask what the unintended consequences of the reform are. The open nature of voting by mail moves away from the secret ballot. Mailing a ballot to an individual's home could possibly affect other types of political participation. For example, some churches in Oregon invite members to come to church on Sunday night and discuss the issues and candidates and mark their ballots together (Dreker 1998). In doing away with the secret ballot, this reform may create an institutional structure that promotes political discussion. The reform offers a contemporary test of whether institutional reforms can increase political discussion, a type of political engagement in social networks. If the reform encourages political discussion, this supports the endogenous thesis, rather than exogenous view of social networks.

Due to the open nature of voting by mail, this might produce situations where people are able to discuss their vote choices. The ballots are mailed to each house three weeks before the elections. Some say that the extra time, availability of additional sources of information when making one's vote decision, and the ability to discuss your choice while voting may provoke more political discussion. The increased exposure to political discussion that may come from this mechanical change in the style of voting might have more than its intended consequences. Democracy is more responsive if the populace is more engaged (Putnam 1993). But what if the structure through which people participate is changed to expose them to more information in a longer, more deliberative context? An institutional change in the method of participation would create a more engaged populace. If the reform creates a new style of participation that is engaging by its structure, then social networking can be encouraged in a top-down approach.

Summary of Central Findings

I now summarize the findings of the book by chapter.

Ch 2. Discussion and Rationality

First, I test the influence of social networks on rational decision-making using an experiment. The experiment uses Tversky and Kahneman's (1983) logic question that examines the conjunction fallacy. I randomly assigned 220 participants from diverse backgrounds to zero-history groups of five discussants; each was placed into one of four conditions. The participants first answer the logic question alone and then in groups with randomly selected leaders. In all conditions, one member of each group was randomly assigned to be the group's leader. In two cases, this leader was chosen randomly from those who had answered the question correctly, and in the other two from those who answered it incorrectly. In one of the correct-answer conditions, leaders were given additional information that promoted the conjunction fallacy, and in one of the incorrect-answer conditions, leaders were given information that would correct the fallacy. I then evaluated both group-level decisions and, separately, individual-level decisions. I find that discussion greatly improves decision-making. I also find that groups with leaders conform to their leaders' beliefs. If the leader correctly answered the conjunction fallacy question, then group members are also more likely to resolve the conjunction fallacy. In groups where the leader was incorrect, group members are more likely to answer incorrectly. Yet in all groups group decision-making is more rational than individuals deciding alone. This shows that even in realistic situations which have leaders trying to sway groups, decision-making is better with discussion than without it.

Ch 3. The Social Basis of Voting Correctly

While the lab results show that in controlled conditions, discussion facilitates rational choice, do these results apply more broadly to the general population? A large literature has established that people learn from political discussion, and some scholars suggest that people will make better choices if they engage in political discussion with opinion leaders. To establish that discussion promotes better vote choices, however, we have to create a measure of rational choice to test the impact of discussion. Recently, scholars have used Lau and Redlawsk's voting correctly measure to test the impact of various influences on the rationality of vote choice. Using this new measure of rationality (voting correctly). I determine whether political discussion has the predicted positive impact. To test this theory, I use 2000 American National Election Study survey data, and show that greater political discussion with knowledgeable discussants leads to more correct voting. This shows that vote by mail may lead to better choices from citizens, because they may get helpful advice when filling out their ballot.

Ch. 4 Influences on Vote Choice in Discussion Networks

After having shown that social networking has a powerful influence on voters' rationality, I further investigate the mechanisms of network influence. Recent research shows that one member's influence is highly dependent on the others in the network, i.e., autoregressive. I test whether the influence of social network political knowledge is also autoregressive. I show that a strong predictor of vote choice similarity is the level of knowledge of the discussant, but greater knowledge of the other network members lessens dyadic agreement. I find that in the 2000 United States Presidential election, having a knowledgeable discussant increases the chance of vote similarity with that discussant by five percentage points, but vote similarity decreases by ten percentage points for each level of residual network knowledge. This research confirms the autoregressive influence of social network political knowledge.

Ch. 5 Policy Opinions and Discussion Networks

I then research how people form policy preferences in discussion networks. A large literature stresses the non-rational nature of decision making. Rational policy preferences require learning specific details in a competitive political environment. Yet, research shows that most people do not have the skills to understand policy and its outcomes. One way people can understand policy is through help from their social networks. Social network influence on policy preference, however, is largely ignored. This research tests the impact from political discussion in social networks on policy preference. I show that the likelihood of supporting a policy increases when one's social network members also support that policy, while controlling for the political knowledge of the respondent, network heterogeneity and size, partisanship, ideology, socioeconomic, and policy specific determinants.

Ch 6. Rational Patriotism and Social Networking

I follow up the policy chapter, by investigating one of the hardest beliefs for the public to be rational about: patriotism. I show that there are two types of patriotism: a rational constructive type and an irrational blind type. I show how social networking promotes the rational type of patriotism, by exposing members to necessary information about the country's problems. I also show a bi-causal relationship between these beliefs and actions. I use a structural equation model of survey data from the 2004 American National Election Studies. The findings show that constructive patriotism promotes social networking, and that social networking separately increases constructive patriotism. Conversely, I also find that blind patriotism lowers social networking, and that social networking lowers blind feelings. This research provides a fuller picture of the relationship of patriotism with social networking than has been provided previously in political theory or political psychology.

Ch 7. What Promotes Political Discussion and Advocacy?

After demonstrating the beneficial impact of interpersonal communication, I turn to understanding what promotes deliberative encounters. Political discussion research often focuses on general discussion without analyzing interesting subsets of interpersonal communication, such as political advocacy. Political advocacy is crucial to study because it is where citizens make clear statements of their beliefs when trying to influence others, which democratic theorists cite as valuable in creating better decision-making in discussion networks. In this chapter, I test theoretically relevant determinants of political advocacy, focusing on campaign spending. Using multilevel logistic regression models of American National Election Study survey data from presidential elections from 1976-2008, I find that campaign spending correlates with an increase in the likelihood of advocating. Additionally, I break these results down by party spending and party identification, and find differentiated results by party. Generally, these results show how the electoral environment shapes interpersonal communication.

Ch 8. The Electoral System and Political Discussion

I then study a fascinating change in the electoral system to see if that has an impact on the level of discussion. Critics of voting by mail express concern over its impact on civil society. For example, Thompson (2004) posits that voting by mail limits electoral civic engagement by preventing the temporal norm of simultaneity on Election Day. I, however, find that the open ballot system of voting by mail promotes political discussion, which I show above leads to better choices. This study tests whether voting by mail increases political discussion by creating a Poisson regression model of NES survey data. The findings show that voting by mail leads to more political discussion, while controlling for political interest, party ID, mobilization, media exposure, feelings of efficacy, and socioeconomic differences. This evidence supports the theory that voting by mail offers voters a more open and deliberatory system.

Ch. 9 Conclusion

In the conclusion, I summarize the results of the book and address how these ideas inform our theoretical understanding of network influence on political rationality.

Chapter 2
Hierarchy, Discussion, and Rationality[*]

Interpersonal communication is foundational to all theories of democracy (Habermas 1984). From Aristotle onwards (Balme 1991), interpersonal communication is given as a chief explanation of human success vis-à-vis other animals (Richerson and Boyd 2004). Modern political science has seen a vast expansion of literature that examines formal interpersonal communication and social networks more generally. Yet, some doubt its beneficial impact due to hierarchy within discursive networks. They reason that beneficial deliberation requires open and frank discussion from all who want to contribute, but hierarchy may silence some voices who defer to the leader. The worry is in real-life situations power inequities are commonplace. These power inequities may silence some voices, leading to sub-optimal decisions, and, further, those who are silenced will be from politically relevant or socially less-powerful groups. If so, interpersonal communication may sometimes be a form of domination, where the less powerful are obliged to consent to what they may not want.

Designers of deliberative events strive to eliminate hierarchy in their discussion groups based on the untested assumption that it will be detrimental to the outcome, but real-world groups often have leaders. Juries have foremen, councils and committees have chairs, and so on. The omitted variable of hierarchy may affect the theorized beneficial effects of interpersonal communication. These critics argue that ignoring hierarchy may greatly overstate the benefits of interpersonal communication. Since no one can deny the importance of interpersonal communication to democracy or the prevalence of hierarchy in human relationships, the role of hierarchy in interpersonal communication needs

* This chapter was co-authored with Sarah Brosnan.

rigorous empirical study. To test whether the benefits of group decision-making hold in hierarchical groups, I manipulated social hierarchy within discusson groups to observe human social interaction in a way not previously envisioned.

Specifically, I test rational group decision-making in an experiment where participants first answer a logic question alone and then in groups with randomly selected leaders. The logic question was constructed by Tversky and Kahneman (1983) to stimulate the conjunction fallacy, which is a common cognitive error in human decision-making. Previous research finds participants solve Tversky and Kahneman's cognitive fallacies more rationally when they discuss it in a group than when they answer it alone (e.g., Druckman 2004). The influence of hierarchy within such groups, however, remains unknown. To test the influence of hierarchy, I randomly assigned 220 participants to zero-history groups of five discussants. Groups were divided into four conditions, under which one member was randomly assigned to be the group's leader. In two conditions, leaders were randomly chosen from among those individuals who had correctly answered the conjunction fallacy question in a pre-test, while in the other two, leaders were chosen from among those who had answered it incorrectly. In one of the correct-answer conditions, leaders were given additional information that promoted the conjunction fallacy. In one of the incorrect-answer conditions, leaders were given information that would correct the fallacy (thus there were four conditions that varied on the dimensions of previous response and additional information provided). Participants were incentivized to give the correct response in their individual responses, by giving participants $10 for a correct response. I then evaluated the rationality of the individual participant's decisions and, separately, groups-level decisions.

I find that people in groups in all conditions decide more rationally after discussion. I also find that those with leaders do conform to their leaders' beliefs. If the leader was able to resolve the conjunction fallacy question, then group members are also more likely to change their answer to a correct answer. In groups where the leader was incorrect, group members are more to likely to change their answer to an incorrect answer as well, but crucially these groups are still are more rational than when deciding alone. Thus, group decision-making is benefited by hierarchy when the leader is correct, but harmed when the group leader is incorrect, but in all cases beneficial. Further analysis using social network techniques shows that the greater persuasiveness that leaders exhibit is due solely to the person being randomly assigned to be the leader, and not due to some other factor, including augmentative persuasion (see in-depth discussion of this below). I also find that leaders from socially powerful groups (whites and males) have disproportionately greater influence than leaders from less socially powerful groups.

Researching hierarchy is important because without it, interpersonal communication is generally found to have a positive influence on group decision-making (e.g., Barabas 2004; or Lupia and McCubbins 2000). For example, Gastil and Dillard (1999) show that discussion in small groups with disagreeing others increases public opinion quality. Fishkin and Luskin (2005, p. 1) summarize their many experiments with deliberative polling by saying that the results from these studies "show that ordinary people can deliberate, that they benefit from doing so, and that the process neither biases nor polarizes their opinions." In addition, Druckman (2004) shows that Tversky and Kahneman's equivalency framing effects are not robust to participants who are allowed to deliberate. Most related to this research, Charness, Karni, and Levin (2010) show that interpersonal communication in leaderless groups helps individuals resolve the conjunction fallacy, using the same question that I test here. Even in this experiment, I find that in all conditions interpersonal communication improves individuals' logic problem-solving skills when compared to the same individuals deciding alone.

Hierarchy, however, is common in real-world interpersonal communication. Although deliberative polling studies do not allow group leaders (and even have facilitators to prevent some members from dominating the group) (Fishkin and Ackerman [2004]), many other forms of interpersonal communication do have leaders. Skocpol (2003) details how pervasive hierarchies are in modern NGOs, which often claim to use interpersonal communication to address social needs. She shows that the "raucous conflict" necessary for a vibrant deliberative democracy has been curtailed by the stifling careerism and cooption of these groups' leaders, and suggests that less hierarchical forms of group governance would lead to more deliberative decision-making. Moreover, we know that an individual's sense of power within a group is highly predictive of their influence in formal groups (Chen, et al. 2009; Anderson, et al. 2006). Furthermore, Anderson and Srivastava (2011) show that members of groups regularly assign power status to group members. Thus, members of groups regularly perceive and respond to hierarchy, but I do not know how this interacts with deliberative performance. As Karpowitz and Mendelberg (2006 p. 645) say "we cannot fully capture the value—or the potential pitfalls—of interpersonal communication without thinking seriously about the social and psychological processes that occur when individuals interact in group settings."

Outside formalized groups, we know that everyday social interactions greatly influence behavior (Huckfeldt 2001; Klofstad 2007; McClurg 2006; Mutz and Mondak 2006), in ways often beneficial for decision-making (Sokhey and Djupe 2011). For example, Eveland and Hively (2009) show that discussion frequency, network size, and some types of network heterogeneity increase political knowledge. And although the tendency for homophily reduces exposure to disagreement, some disagreement is still often encountered, with beneficial effects (Price, Cappella, and Nir 2002, Nir 2011). Nevertheless, Blau's (1964) social exchange theory suggests that we can expect hierarchy to be common even in informal advice networks because people seek out the powerful for advice to get into their superior's network. We have almost no research in political science on whether the positive influence of discussion continues when discussing informally with bosses and other social superiors, but Ryan (2010) finds that the impact of an opinion leader's partisanship is a greater influence on their discussants than their actual knowledge. Crucially, this shows the social transfer of knowledge is not the sole factor in discussion, and suggests that the powerful will be able to sway the less powerful in ways beyond rational argumentation. Thus, because formalized deliberative groups often have leaders, and once outside formalized groups we can expect social hierarchy in human relations, this omitted variable is crucial for understanding interpersonal communication, one of democracy's foundational concepts.

Power in Group Decision-making

Deliberation is central to modern theories of democracy (Bohman 1996; Fishkin 1991; Dryzek 1990). While interpersonal communication is common (with Jacobs, Cook and Delli Caprini 2009 finding that 25 percent of American survey respondents say they have attended a public meeting or hearing in the last year), the positive impact of group interpersonal communication may be valid only in the absence of power differentials among discussants. There is an important theoretical debate on power differentials in interpersonal communication. Many critiques of deliberative democracy argue that power will usually be unevenly distributed in discussion (such as critiques of Habermas in Foucault 2002). This is a crucial potential flaw in deliberative democracy that has been explicated by both feminist and poststructuralist critiques of deliberative democracy (see Cohen and Arato 1992). Even though theorists and practitioners try to eliminate some of the raw power differentials by having structured norms of equality and mutual respect, the underlying problem of power differences between discussants in real-life formal settings remains (see Ackerman and Fishkin 2004 for more on some specific procedures).

To give an example, when men and women debate, it is possible that men will gain acquiescence from women by "winning" the debate, which may seem to be a fair way to resolve conflict (Frazer 1992). If, however, the men win the debate and gain the outcome they desire due to social customs that promote male hierarchical dominance, then this is not a fair process and decision-making by group discussion merely tricks women into submission (Frazer 1992). Critically, these power inequities may create sub-optimal group decisions. Yet, there has been little formal, empirical testing of these critiques with clearly articulated hypotheses in controlled experimental conditions (although Mendelberg and Karpowitz [2007] test the impact of group gender composition). And I know that jury members higher in socioeconomic status have a greater influence, even with incorrect arguments (Hastie, Penrod, and Pennington 1983). Furthermore, these critiques may not go far enough as they do not take seriously the cultural differences that may lead to differential influences of hierarchy across different cultures (Richey 2009). As we know that groups commonly have leaders, this aspect of groups should be incorporated into research on interpersonal communication. While past research provides evidence of the benefits of group decision-making, much of it does not examine other common social forces in groups, such as the relative power of the discussants. Thus, additional experiments are needed.

In addition, Lazega (1992) details another weapon that hierarchal elites use to gain suasion in small groups. Group leaders disproportionately make "knowledge claims" that only they have access to based on their position of power. For example, a chair of a committee could manipulate the decision by claiming to have knowledge of what the mayor/dean/director really wants. Since it is plausible that this leader spoke with higher-ups, this knowledge claim will win many debates. But since only the leader can plausibly make this claim, which is often unverifiable, the leader could simply be lying, exaggerating, or cherry-picking the evidence to ensure they get their preferred outcome. Lazega (1992) finds that these claims are common and have a strong impact on group decision-making. This fascinating analysis of the sociology of power in groups has not been tested in political science. To ensure that I am accurately measuring the behavior of leaders in our experimental groups, I create additional conditions where leaders can plausibly make knowledge claims, which I expect will increase their influence. Intentionally, the leaders in one condition were given inaccurate information designed to promote the conjunction fallacy, while those in another condition were given knowledge that corrects this fallacy.

The Conjunction Fallacy

To test whether or not groups can make a correct decision, I will use a commonly used logic question from cognitive psychology, on the conjunction fallacy. It is derived from Tversky and Kahneman (1983). In their experiment, subjects were asked to read the following and rank which choice is more probable: Linda is thirty one years old, single, outspoken, and very bright. She majored in philosophy. As a student, she was deeply concerned with issues of discrimination and social justice, and also participated in anti-nuclear demonstrations. Which is more probable? A. Linda is a bank teller, or B. Linda is a bank teller and is active in the feminist movement.

The original Tversky and Kahneman (1983) experiment (subsequently replicated across many samples) shows that over 70 percent of subjects incorrectly chose sequence B, since Linda resembles an active feminist more than she resembles a bank teller. However, sequence A is superior to B, because sequence A is included in B. B (Linda is a bank teller and is active in the feminist movement) is just A (Linda is a bank teller) with an additional condition (is active in the feminist movement). Thus, this question tests the conjunction fallacy that is formally defined as, for all A and B, $P(B\&A)$ $P(A)$. Since the probability that A and B are simultaneously true is always less than or equal to the probability that A is true, sequence B cannot be more likely than sequence A. The common explanation for this fallacy is that the participant is influenced by the representativeness heuristic. The details given about Linda's college days makes

Linda resemble the representative heuristics of feminists more than bank teller, so subjects are primed to reach an irrational conclusion.

This logic question was chosen to test group decision-making for three important reasons. First, there is an objectively correct answer. Other possible topics such as public policy debates will not allow us to examine the role of the group leader in providing incorrect information, as it would be difficult to find an a priori correct answer for these policy decisions, unless they are artificial replications of these cognitive fallacies, such as alternative questions from Tversky and Kahneman. Additionally, the conjunction fallacy plagues decision-making in a variety of important real-world situations. Gaining data on its spread in public discussion is valuable. Finally, previous research on group decision-making has used this question (e.g., Charness, Karni, and Levin 2010), thus, the ideas and measures I use in our experiment have been pre-tested and validated by others, and are comparable to the existing literature.

Hypotheses

My aim is to investigate the role of group discussion on rational decision-making. First, I hypothesize that group discussion will benefit decision-making for individuals. Specifically I predict that:

H1: Discussion will lead to more rational choices on average.

We also want to test the impact of hierarchy, to see if deliberation under real-life constraints also has beneficial effects.

H2a: Participants with a correct leader will change at greater rates to a correct response when compared to those with an incorrect leader.

I further test Lazega's (1992) "knowledge claims" idea by giving leaders additional information designed to resolve or promote the conjunction fallacy, to determine whether this increases the influence on group decision-making.

H2b: Participants with a leader who is given additional information about the conjunction fallacy will change their answer to match their leader at a greater rate than those participants with leaders not given information

I also want to see if the leader's decision-making alters the group as a whole. Thus, I also investigate the same hypotheses at the group level, where I determine what the group chose, by using a majority-rule decision-making process where I determine the choices of a majority of the participants in each group before and after discussion.

H3a: A majority of members in groups with a correct leader will change at greater rates to a correct response as compared to a majority of members in groups with an incorrect leader.

H3b: A majority of group members with a leader who is given additional information about the conjunction fallacy will change their answer to match their leader at a greater rate than a majority of group members with leaders not given information

I also want to see if leaders who are from socially powerful groups will have a disproportionately large influence. The most common critique of deliberative democracy is that visual cues of power such as race or being male will create deference to these people from those from socially less-powerful groups (e.g., Young 2000). I can easily determine if this is true by examining two easy-to-see characteristics of belonging to socially powerful groups: race and gender. Being of the white race or being male should represent the most powerful categories from these identities. All participants will know if their leaders are male or white, whereas other aspects of power such as income are more subtle and may not be apparent at first. I will use the pre-test questionnaire data on race and gender to determine if being white or male gives these leaders greater influence than female or non-white leaders.

H3a: Male leaders will persuade more of their group to change positions to match their answer than female leaders

H3b: White leaders will persuade more of their group to change positions to match their answer than non-white leaders.

Experimental Procedures

Small group research has a long history of influencing our understanding of political behavior (see Verba 1961). The small groups I constructed are very similar to groups constructed for deliberative polling and other deliberative events. To investigate the role of hierarchy in group decision-making, I conducted an experiment on a convenience sample of 220 undergraduates at a large public research university in the southeastern United States. Participants were given $10 to participate. Participants first answered a questionnaire that contained demographic information, and the conjunction fallacy question from Tversky and Kahneman (1983) that was described above (Linda is a bank teller), after which they handed in their questionnaire. Importantly, this pre-experiment questionnaire allows us to know whether the participant is influenced by their group, because I know how they answered the logic question before discussion. After participants answered the logic question alone, they were assigned to groups of five. All groups were told to discuss the same logic question again with members of their group, and answer it again after twenty minutes of discussion. They were told that if they answered it correctly the second time, they would receive an additional $10.

To test the influence of hierarchy, the groups were divided into four experimental conditions. In conditions 1 and 3, a randomly selected member was chosen to be the group leader from among the set who had answered the question correctly the first time. The leader was appointed by the experimenter telling the group that this person was their leader (see script in Appendix). The leaders were told to explain their logic for answering the question to the group. In condition 2 and 4, the leader was chosen from among the set that had answered the question incorrectly in the pre-test. The leaders were appointed in the same way (using the same script) and again were told to explain their logic to their group.

Here is a summary of the conditions:

• Correct Leader Condition: The experimenter selected a member of the discussion group to be the group leader. The group was instructed that this person is the group's leader. The group leader was randomly chosen from the subset that correctly answered the logic question in a pre-test questionnaire (but neither the group nor the leaders were informed of the criterion).

• Incorrect Leader Condition: The experimenter selected a member of the discussion group to be the group leader. The group is informed as in condition one. The group leader was randomly chosen from the subset that incorrectly answered the logic question in a pre-test questionnaire.

• Correct Leader plus Correct Information Condition: The experimenter selected a member of the discussion group to be the group leader. The group was instructed that this person is the group's leader. The group leader was randomly chosen from the subset that correctly answered the logic question in a pre-test questionnaire and allowed to read additional information designed to solve the conjunction fallacy (described below).

• Incorrect Leader plus Incorrect Information Condition: The experimenter selected a member of the discussion group to be the group leader. The group is informed as in condition one. The group leader was randomly chosen from the subset that incorrectly answered the logic question in a pre-test questionnaire and allowed to read additional information designed to promote the conjunction fallacy (described below).

The leader was selected in private, without the participants seeing how or why they were selected, in between the pre-test and the group discussion. The group leaders were told to explain their logic to the group orally. After twenty minutes of discussion, the participants were given the final questionnaire and instructed to write the answer that they believe correct. The participants also answered an open-ended question on why they chose their answer. This allows us to track the influence of hierarchy, by tracking the spread of correct and incorrect influence on decision-making.

To create a credible knowledge claim, in front of the other group members, only the leaders in Correct Leader plus Correct Information Condition were handed a sheet of paper that said "Linda is more likely to be a bank teller than she is to be a feminist bank teller, because every bank teller is a bank teller, but some women bank tellers are not feminist, and Linda could be one of them." This explains the conjunction fallacy. After the leader read the sheet of paper, they were asked if they understood it (all said they understood it), and it was taken away. Similarly, in the Incorrect Leader plus Incorrect Information Condition, only the leaders were given a sheet of paper that said "Linda is more likely to be a feminist bank teller than she is to be a bank teller, because she resembles an active feminist more than she resembles a bank teller." This promotes the conjunction fallacy, and they were asked if they understood it (all said they understood it), and it was taken away. Because the other members saw them handed this sheet of paper, the leaders' explanation of the logic from the paper handout will be a credible knowledge claim, and allow us to test this common feature of power in interpersonal communication, as described by Lazega (1992).

Data and Results

The sample was selected from a university-wide mandatory introductory course in American politics at a large public university in the Southeastern United States. It matched the demographics of the university closely. It was 68 percent female, with an average age of nineteen. Racially, it was 13 percent Asian, 50 percent black, 28 percent white, and 8 percent other race. It contained students from thirty two majors. This diverse sample provides an excellent understanding of decision making among diverse groups of people, as are present in real-world situations. The participants were selected to come from different classes, and each was asked if they knew any other members. All participants reported having no familiarity with their group members, so these are so-called zero-history groups, which are commonly used in research on group decision-making (for example, see Gastil, Black, and Moscovitz 2008).

I used the answers from the pre-test questionnaire, which was answered alone before group discussion, to determine how discussion changes the participant's answer. For groups without a leader, 22 percent of participants answered the conjunction fallacy question correctly, and after discussion 56 percent did so (difference significant at $p < 0.000$). 37 percent moved from an incorrect answer to a correct answer, while only 2 percent moved from correct to incorrect. This is major finding in that it shows under controlled experimental conditions, a majority got the correct answer after discussion, whereas only a small minority did so before discussion. This confirms the central premise of this book: discussion leads to more rational choices.

To test the group-level hypothesis, I created a group-level dichotomous variable that measured change at the group level. To do this requires two steps; first, I created a variable that measured whether a majority of the participants who will be in the group answered correctly or not in the pre-test, where it was coded (1) if a majority answered correctly and (0) if a majority answered incorrectly. Similarly, I also aggregated the post-treatment answers for majorities within the groups. The pre-treatment group variable was then subtracted from the post-treatment group variable to create a measurement of group-level change. Across all treatments, before discussion 26 percent of groups had a majority of their participants answer it correctly, and after discussion 58 percent did (difference significant at $p < 0.000$). Discussion changed the distribution so that in a total of 33 percent groups, a majority of participants changed to a correct answer. In fact, zero groups moved to an incorrect majority. With either way of measuring impact, discussion greatly benefitted decision-making.

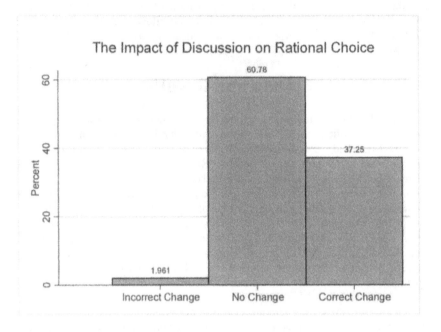

Figure 2.1: This bar graph compares levels of the three types of change from the individual answer to the group answer.

Although conducted under different experimental conditions, these results basically replicate studies such as Druckman (2004) and Charness, Karni, and Levin (2010), which find that the Tversky and Kahneman critique of human decision-making is a function of forcing participants to decide in an atomistic solo fashion. Once participants are allowed to decide in a realistic fashion with the help of others, then decision-making radically improves.

Now let's examine the groups randomly assigned a leader. Amazingly, even with half of the groups assigned incorrect leaders, interpersonal communication still resulted in a majority of groups getting it right, showing the clear benefits of group decision-making. I hypothesized that leaders have an influence over their group's members, affecting decision-making. In particular, I predicted that participants in groups whose leaders were correct should have more correct answers than those in groups with incorrect leaders. These predictions were supported by these data (see figure 2.2). Individuals in the correct leader condition increased the percentage who correctly answered after discussion by 47.5 percent. Individuals in the incorrect leader condition were also more likely to arrive at the correct answer after discussion. However, the degree to which they improved (19.6 percent) was far less than individuals in the correction condition (47.5% vs. 19.6% correct, difference p < 0.000). It is interesting that discussion is beneficial in all treatments, however clearly it is much less beneficial when a leader is incorrect. I find less support for the idea that leaders with credible claims to exclusively held knowledge had greater influence. I see significant effects between these conditions (52.5% and 15.5% correct, difference $p < 0.000$), but they are not statistically significantly different from leaders without additional correct information. Since both are signed in expected directions, this could be due to statistical power issues.

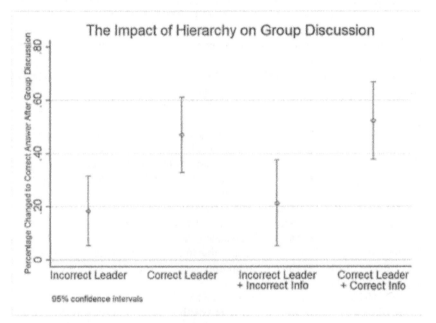

Figure 2.2: This graph shows average improvement for individuals in answering the conjunction fallacy question after group discussion across the four experimental conditions.

This shows that being in the correct leader condition leads to a greater likelihood of a majority group members answering correctly, while having an incorrect leader lowered this likelihood (58.2% and 36.0% correct, difference $p < 0.000$). Again, the additional information treatments had significant effects that were not significantly different from similar leaders without additional information given (68.6% and 21.9% correct, difference $p < 0.000$). This shows that the individual effects found in figure 2.1 are replicated in group-level effects.

Some may wonder if adding another correct or incorrect member to any discussion group will increase the likelihood of the other members answering in a similar way. If this critique is true, then the effects shown above are merely from the leader convincing others in their group through arguments (or charisma or some other factor) rather than deference to power. There is an easy statistical test to determine if this is so. We can create a dyadic social network data set, where each group member is tied to every other member in his or her group. In this case, each participant is paired with each of their four discussion partners in their group. Since every group has five members, there will be four partners for each member—termed a "discussant." These dyadic data are often used in research on political discussion (e.g., Richey 2008). Since in any group there are four discussants, I can see if those who are leaders have a disproportionate influence when compared to others in the group who have a similar opinion.

I created a logistic regression model on these data, where the standard errors are clustered for member. The dependent variable Persuasion is whether the participant changes their opinion from the pre-test logic question to match that of their discussant, coded (1) if so and (0) if not. I create a variable for whether the discussant was a Leader (coded 1), or not (coded 0), and a control variable for the discussant's answer on the logic question coded (1) if Correct answer and (0) if not.

This result shows that leaders have a disproportionate influence on group members regardless of the nature of their opinions. I find that randomly assigned leaders are significantly more likely to have their partner change their pre-test answer to be in line with their opinion, while holding the actual opinion on the logic question constant. Clarify estimates show this to be about a nine percentage point increase in the likelihood of dyadic matching. Because these are randomly selected leaders, they will not have superior argumentation, charisma, or anything else that could persuade when compared to those not randomly-selected, as these factors will balance due to unit homogeneity. This is powerful evidence that leaders have disproportionate influence over groups not due to any other factor than being a leader.

Using these same dyadic pair data and Persuasion dependent variable, I test predictions 3a and 3b, to determine whether white or male leaders have a disproportionately large influence over their group members. In the pre-test questionnaire, I asked the race (Asian, Black or African American, other race, or white) and gender of each participant. These models interact gender or race with being a leader. In model 1, white leaders have a statistically significantly greater influence than the omitted category of Black leaders, while model 2 shows a similar greater influence for male leaders. This implies that social hierarchy will influence group decision-making by both assignment to power by officials (as I did when I randomly assigned these leaders), and by belonging to powerful social groups. These results suggest that interpersonal communication will be riddled with hierarchy even when attempts are made to explicitly exclude it, because some members belong to hierarchically superior groups.

Conclusion

The results show that rational decision-making flows out of interpersonal communication. Deliberation is crucial to understanding human accomplishment, and I find that it is not moderated by hierarchy to the extent that it eliminates its effectiveness. I find that the effect of hierarchy will be beneficial if the leader is correct, which cannot be assumed when designing deliberative bodies. This research suggests that the public has the ability to use interpersonal communication to make better decisions. Improving democratic practices is crucial for advanced industrial nations (Putnam 2007).

I found that interpersonal communication in all conditions was superior to decision-making alone, and this included conditions in which the leaders were incorrect and given additional incorrect information. In all conditions, group interpersonal communication is superior to individual decision-making, while hierarchy moderates some of these benefits of interpersonal communication. Gaining knowledge about the impact of power relations in social interaction may allow insights that facilitate better policies on deliberative forums. If the impact of unequal power in discussion networks within deliberative public forums is known, this knowledge can result in effective public discussion. Determining the impact of group power relations tells us how to provide an environment that is conducive to successfully using interpersonal communication. For example, policy-makers and activists can sponsor deliberative opportunities with more emphasis on actively ensuring that equal power in the discussion is given to all participants.

Chapter 3
The Social Basis of Voting Correctly

After having established that political discussion increases rationality in logic questions, I now turn to examine whether that beneficial effect applies outside the lab. The next central question to address is whether voters who have political discussions more often will vote more rationally. Citizens often behave in ways that appear irrational (Achen and Bartels 2004, Bartels 1996, 2005). Many pundits, theorists, and scholars posit that if citizens discuss politics more, we will have a better democracy (see Bohman [1998] for a review). A large literature has established that people learn from social networks (Berelson, Lazarsfeld, and McPhee 1954; Brown and Brown 2003; Linimon and Joslyn 2002; Katz and Lazarfeld 1955; McAdam and Paulsen 1993; Price, Capella, and Nir 2002), and the logic follows that we could improve democracy if people only had more, and better, political discussion. The unstated assumption being that better understanding equates to rational choices. Under strict conditions, formal interpersonal communication has been shown to educate (Barabas 2004), but informal political discussion is more common, and is an efficient division of labor (Conover, Johnston, Searing, and Crewe 2002). Research has shown that in everyday conversation, opinion leaders teach their associates about politics (Huckfeldt 2001), and that informal political discussion is not rare (e.g., see Huckfeldt, Pappi, and Ikeda 2005). This literature finds that political discussion with knowledgeable people increases knowledge of politics. Thus it seems plausible that if people receive advice on candidates from knowledgeable discussants it will help them chose the candidate that better reflects their vision of how government should act.

But showing discussion increases knowledge does not show that rational choices flow from getting political advice. Choice requires both information and information processing, and the latter is often untested in current social network research. To establish that discussion promotes rational vote choices, we have to establish a criterion for rational choice and test it. Lau and Redlawsk (1997, 2006) create a measure of rational vote choice, termed voting correctly. Recently, scholars have used the voting correctly measure to test the impact of various influences on the quality of the electorate. For example, Baum and Jamison (2006) show that watching candidates speak on daytime talk shows helps low-information voters vote correctly, because it educates them about the candidates' beliefs. With this new measure of rationality—of how well choices match preferences—we can determine if political discussion has the predicted effects. To test this effect, I use 2000 American National Election Study survey data, which has information on vote choice, political preferences, and discussion in social networks. The results show that greater political discussion with knowledgeable discussants does lead to more correct voting.

This research has both important policy and theoretical contributions. For policy, if more discussion creates a better electorate, then this provides strong evidence in support of reforms—such as increased civic education—that instill the virtues of political discussion. Also, other proposed reforms can be created with an eye toward increasing political discussion. If, however, political discussion does not create better choices, then we must rethink ways to improve rationality, if possible, and question the role of discussion in democracy. Theoretically, this research helps to answer a crucial question of political behavior, the paradox of mass democracy (Neuman 1986). Taber (2003) calls this paradox the most important question for political behavior research. Simply, the paradox is how democracy is so successful, when citizens are so inept. The lack of political knowledge is well known (Althaus 1998, Alverez 1998, Delli Caprini and Ketter 1996). But the limitations on rational choice go beyond a simple lack of knowledge, and include cognitive limitations. For example, given simple problems, most people can be easily manipulated in predictable ways, such as risk aversion (Kahneman and Tversky 1979). How then does democracy succeed, when citizens cannot make the simplest choices rationally?

Druckman (2004) makes an important contribution in solving this paradox, by showing that when individuals make decisions solo, these mistakes are common. If, however, people are allowed to discuss their information, they are far less likely to fall into these common intellectual traps. In particular, if people with diverse information can communicate, these biases all but disappear. It is important, then, not to base research on atomistic views of political animals. By incorporating social networking into research on rationality, we can more realistically model decision-making, which is often done with help from friends and family (Mendelberg 2005). Based on this research, it is important to see how many people take advantage of political discussion, and whether this translates into rational vote choice.

These experiments provide evidence of the benefits of discussion, but they do not prove that political discussion during a competitive election will improve rationality. Campaign manipulation of voters' emotions is well known. No one in the Druckman (2004) study, for example, was maliciously advocating that the group choose irrationally. Yet, this is precisely what happens during elections when campaigns woo voters. Campaigns try to sway some voters away from choosing rationally, to win their votes. Thus, while this experiential evidence is very beneficial, it needs to be tested in a real-world election to establish external validity.

Data

I test the impact of social networks using NES data from 2000. The 2000 NES had a response rate of 86 percent with 1807 respondents (see Appendix Table 1 for a table of summary statistics for these data).

Dependent Variable: Voting Correctly

Lau and Redlawsk (1997, 2006) develop a sophisticated amalgam of beliefs about politics that can be used to determine if someone actually votes for the candidate that best matches their preferences. In this definition, rationality occurs when voters choose the candidate who matches their preferences most. They are voting correctly if they choose the most similar candidate. The quick and easy assumption often made by rational choice scholars that all people vote for the most similar candidate ignores the costs of information processing (Lau 2003). Further, campaigns manipulate and confuse voters to vote against their preferences. Note that rationality is not defined as choosing who we think is appropriate for the voter, because we cannot assume we know what is in the voter's best interest. Democratic theory, however, requires that the voter choose coherently with their preferences. This straightforward definition of rationality does not impose any normative constraints, other than that people choose who they think matches their preferences best.

While this definition of rationality is straightforward, by necessity the construction of the measure is not. I cannot simply match ideology with vote choice and call it rational, because this makes a normative assertion that issue voting is all that matters. Supporting a candidate from one's social groups, candidate competence and performance ability, and building a party by supporting a disliked candidate are all rational political concerns. The test of rationality must allow for these other considerations when testing the validity of vote choice. The voting correctly measure is sophisticated enough to handle these other concerns.

Basically, there are four aspects in Lau and Redlawsk's test of correct voting. First, they include party identification. Thus, if the voter votes for the candidate of the same party, they are given one point for rationality. Second, they use respondent agreement with the candidates' policy stands, measured using the directional method of Rabinowitz and Macdonald (1989). For exam-

ple, if the respondent is moderately pro-life, then they are given a point for voting correctly if they choose any pro-lifer, even over a moderate pro-choice candidate who may be closer to them on a unidimensional scale. A candidate's support for the policy is determined by what the most knowledgeable respondents
think is the candidate's position on the issue. The knowledgable discussants are
those listed by the survey interviewer as being very knowledgeable about politics. Using the same 2000 NES data, Baum and Allison (2006) verify the validity of this approach, by showing that the assessment of a candidate's policy position by knowledgable survey respondents is similar to those of political experts
that they interview, such as political science professors. This process was com-
pleted for nine policies. Third, they include candidate–social group linkages.
Using the question on closeness to social groups, if Bush voters have a p < 0.05
relationship with a certain group, and the respondent also felt close to this group
and voted for Bush, then they are given one credit toward correct voting. The
groups that were close to Gore were unions, blacks, and women. The groups
close to Bush were southerners, businessmen, and men. Finally they include the
incumbent's job performance. Here I follow Baum and Jamison (2006) and use
Clinton's approval as a proxy for Gore, as there was no incumbent in 2000. All
of these considerations are summed to create a summary evaluation of candidate
preference.

Figure 3.1 shows the summary evaluation for both candidates was basically centered on zero, implying that the closeness of the 2000 election matches
the rational preferences of citizens. Here, a higher score represents that a Bush
vote choice is more rational for the respondent, and a lower score that Gore is a
better choice. Gore is slightly more of an optimal choice for this sample, as the
median summary evaluation is closer to Gore, -.453. This suggests that if this
large random sample is representative of the electorate and this measure is an
accurate test of rationality, then the candidate who won in 2000 was not the
electorate's optimal choice. Also interesting is that this is clearly a normal distribution, suggesting that talk of a polarized electorate—which would have a
bimodal distribution—is not correct in 2000 (see Fiorina, Abrams, and Pope
[2004] for more).

The final step in creating the measure is to code as one every voter who
voted for the candidate that they are closer to on this scale, and a zero for those
who voted for the candidate they are farther away from. For example, everyone
with a positive score is voting correctly if they vote for Bush, and voting incorrectly if they voted for Gore. Using this measure, we see that only around 80
percent of the voters voted correctly in 2000. As most elections are decided by
less than twenty percentage points, including 2000, increased correct voting can
have a massive effect on politics. If the reforms that have been posited lead to
more political discussion that increases correct voting, then they can change
many electoral outcomes.

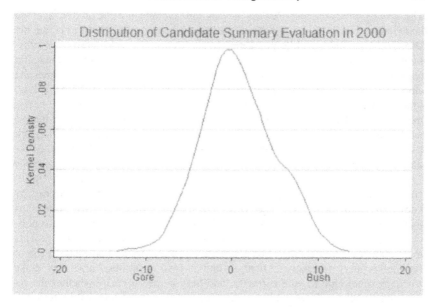

Figure 3.1: This graph shows the summary evaluation of NES 2000 respondents for Bush and Gore in the 2000 elections. See text for details. The plot uses a Gaussian kernel function.

Independent Variable Coding

In 2000, the NES collected social network data by asking the respondents about the people within their network. The NES asked the respondent to describe characteristics about the people with whom the respondent most often has political discussions. This process is called a name generator. Name-generator methodology has allowed scholars to access network information in large random sample surveys, and the validity of this method has been established. For example, Huckfeldt, Sprague, and Levine (2000) use snowball surveys (where the respondents and their network members are surveyed) to obtain objective data on the accuracy of the respondents' interpretations of their discussants' characteristics (see also Ikeda and Huckfeldt 2001). These results show that most people are able to accurately describe their discussants in name-generator surveys. Based on these empirical findings of validity, many researchers use name generators to investigate social networks (see Huckfeldt, Johnson and Sprague 2004, 36).

The key causal variable is created from the perceived level of political knowledge of the social network. The respondent rated the knowledge of each network member from not much (zero), average (one), and a great deal (two).

The discussants are described as having on average a little above average knowledge. The description given in the name generator allows me to create the Discussion quality variable, by summing the knowledge of all network discussants weighted by how often the discussant is spoken to about politics. Thus, if a respondent lists four discussants, I sum the knowledge of each member times the amount of discussion with that member, coded from not much (zero), a little (one), some (two), and a great deal of discussion (three). This allows me to test the impact of discussing politics often with a knowledgeable network, which is what is posited to be needed to improve democracy. In cases where the network has one, two, or three discussants, the measure is created with the same procedure as with four-person networks.

Political and cognitive sophistication from the respondent may influence correct voting. The political knowledge control variable is determined by knowledge of political facts. The NES has a set of political knowledge questions that asked whether or not the respondent knew details about several famous politicians, and these are used to create a measure of political knowledge. This measure sums the total correct responses to questions about a politician's job or state of primary residence. Attention and interest in politics also may make someone more able to vote correctly, and here is measured by whether the respondent is not much (zero), somewhat, (one), or very much (two) interested in politics, multiplied by their level of attention to the 2000 campaign, coded from not much (zero), somewhat, (one), or much attention (two). Ideology is measured on a seven-point scale, with conservative as higher. Partisanship is coded from not attached to any party (zero), slightly (one), somewhat (two), and strongly partisan (three). I follow Baum and Jamison (2006), and include a variable on Media usage, summing whether or not the respondent gets political news from watching television nightly news, newspapers, the Internet, and radio. I also control for being male, white, Hispanic, income in $5,000 categories, education by degree attainment, and age.

As the dependent variable is dichotomous, I use a logistic regression model. As the data is clustered in groups of number of discussants, I follow Huckfeldt, Johnson, and Sprague (2004, 55) and correct the standard errors for clustering (see Rogers 1993).

Results

I show two specifications, one that includes control variables for political sophistication, and another that also includes demographic variables. The logistic regression models in table 3 fit the data well, as Receiver Operator Characteristics diagnostics shows that model 1 explains 83 percent of the variance of the dependent variable, while model 2 explains 86 percent. For the hypothesis tests, discussion quality has a large effect in both models. This confirms the hypothesis that having more discussion with better informed people will lead to more correct voting. Below I examine the impact of each level of quality discussion.

As expected, more attention and interest in politics increases the probability of correct voting. One interesting finding is that news exposure decreases the probability of correct voting. This may be due to bias in the news media, or more exposure to campaign advertising, often consumed with news, that will sway voters against a rational choice.

Table 3.1: The Determinants of Voting Correctly in 2000

Variable	Coef.	(S. E.)	Coef.	(S. E.)
Discussion quality	0.033*	(0.014)	0.043***	(0.004)
Attention and interest	0.464*	(0.204)	0.370+	(0.201)
News exposure	-0.048**	(0.017)	-0.070***	(0.018)
Political knowledge	0.127***	(0.031)	0.089	(0.077)
Partisanship	0.519***	(0.039)	0.560***	(0.046)
Ideology	0.051	(0.052)	0.068	(0.058)
Strength of candidate preference	1.046***	(0.104)	1.227***	(0.228)
Male			0.089	(0.253)
White			-0.894	(0.587)
Income			-0.033	(0.029)
Education			0.248***	(0.077)
Age			0.016	(0.015)
Hispanic			-0.889	(0.789)
Intercept	-0.926	(0.238)	-1.573	(0.359)
Number	850		757	

Table 3.1: Cells represent unstandardized coefficients and standard errors of logistic regression models for determinants of voting correctly in 2000.

Political knowledge has a strong effect in model 1, but when the demographic variables are added, the standard error increases so that it is not significant at the $p < .05$ level. This is probably due to the inclusion of education in the demographic variables. Partisanship shows a massive positive effect on the probability of voting correctly. This matches previous research on the beneficial effects of strong active engaged parties, which can create partisanship (Rosenstone and Hansen 1993). The idea is that active partisanship teaches lessons on how to process political information. As with previous research, I did not find an effect from ideology. The largest effect in both models came from strength of candidate preference. It seems likely that someone needs a reason to strongly like a candidate, and this measure correlates highly with correct voting. Most of the demographic variables had little effect on correct voting. Being male, being white, being Hispanic, level of income, and age had no discernible effect. Education, however, had a large effect. This is intuitive, as education often entails analysis and the promotion of critical thinking.

Also of interest is the relative effect of each level of discussion quality. I use the same control variables as before to measure the impact of increasing quality discussion. Figure 3.2 holds the other independent variables at their mean and predicts the probability of incorrect voting if the amount of quality discussion was one standard deviation below the mean, at the mean level, and one standard deviation above the mean level. This simulation predicts the likelihood of voting incorrectly if a lot of input came from knowledgable discussants compared to little input. A simulated person with one standard deviation less quality discussion has a 17 percent predicted probability of voting incorrectly (standard error .026), someone at the mean level of discussion has a 12 percent predicted probability of voting incorrectly (standard error .013), while holding all else constant. Someone at one standard deviation above the mean is predicted to vote incorrectly 9 percent of the time (standard error .015). A change from one standard deviation below the mean to one standard deviation above the mean, ceteris paribus, results in about one-fourth of a standard deviation increase in correct voting. This change is around eight percentage points, and is significant at the $p < .10$ level. This suggests that social networking is one way in which citizens can improve their understanding of politics and that people can increase political rationality with informal discussion.

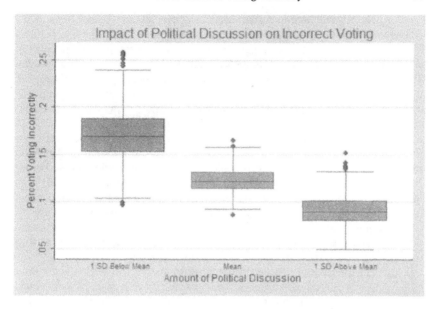

Figure 3.2: This graph shows that more political discussion with knowledgable discussants decreases incorrect voting. The boxes represent the 90 percent confidence intervals for the amount of incorrect voting, while holding all control variables constant, created by Clarify. Calculated from model in Table 3.1, model 2.

Conclusion

We see that in both lab experiments in chapter 2 and nationally representative survey data in this chapter that discussion promotes rational decision-making. Here, I find that more political discussion with knowledgeable discussants increases correct voting. Increasing rationality through discussion has implications for the vote-by-mail reform, which has been shown to boost discussions. I find that the more political discussion people had, the better their choices. The compositional aggregation theory is supported by these results, where discussion in networks increases the rationality of easily swayed citizens. The paradox of mass democracy may be resolved by including the beneficial influence of interpersonal communication on decision-making. Most previous analyses only examined micro- and macro-level influences while ignoring the role of communication in informal networks. As with the experimental evidence of Druckman (2004), I find that during the 2000 elections, discussion lessens irrational behavior.

These results are important because understanding the influence of so-cial networks may allow opportunities to develop programs to increase political knowledge. For example, one suggestion is for government to promote political understanding by sponsoring intergroup interaction (Ackerman and Fishkin 2004; Leib 2004). If programs can be created that sponsor political discussion, they may force people to encounter new ideas and have a large impact on politi-cal behavior. Primary and secondary education has moved away from civic edu-cation, where politics of the United States is a primary focus, to a focus on so-cial groups and world cultures. Some suggest that this had a powerful effect on limiting interest in American politics, and subsequent discussion of American politics (Macedo 2003). If so, then implementing civic education would be one easy reform that can instigate more political discussion. Additionally, it shows that theorists who urge less democratic control, because the masses are incapa-ble of rational behavior (e.g., Lippmann 1924), should not discount the benefits of group decision-making. People do not choose in vacuum, and have access to potentially beneficial discussions. This research supports theorists, such as Put-nam (2000), who want more social interaction to improve democracy.

The question of whether better public discourse will lead to better poli-cy outcomes is central to modern debates over the effectiveness of democracy. For example, Shapiro (1999) critiques discourse scholars for ignoring the power relations that stall needed change. He points to the successful campaign to con-fuse citizens on the effects of universal health care in 1994 as an example of abusive power, not failed discourse. In contrast, this research suggests that if Americans had more and better political discussion over an issue, a more opti-mal decision can come about even in competitive environments, where vested interests are trying to confuse voters. The 2000 campaign featured large manipu-lative campaigns, with intense interest-group lobbying on both sides. Yet, in this environment where power was clearly being used to manipulate opinions, dis-cussion improved correct voting. To take Shapiro's (1999) example, this re-search suggests that if more informal discussion had taken place in 1994, then more optimal outcomes would have been chosen. Thus, more work should focus on how to instigate political discussion.

Chapter 4
Influences on Vote Choice in
Discussion Networks

To further investigate how discussion leads to rational choices, I now examine how political knowledge in social networks influences voters. Research shows that social networking has a powerful influence on voters (Huckfeldt and Sprague 1995). Those knowledgeable about politics are likely to be influential, and if so this may help low information voters choose candidates wisely. Scholars find that perceived political knowledge in social networks does influence vote choice (e.g. Huckfeldt, Ikeda, and Pappi 2000). Yet, current research only examines the direct influence of opinion leaders or cumulative network knowledge. It does not examine the relational level of knowledge between network members in determining influence. But what may be important is how knowledgeable opinion leaders are in comparison to others in the close-tie social network. Importantly, the influence is not simply due to knowledge as in opinion leader theory, but depends on their expertise relative to the other network members. In other words, influence may derive from the perception that one friend is more knowledgeable than the other people we know, not the overall knowledge of the friend per se, or that of the entire network. I predict that opinion leaders will have less influence if their knowledge approximates that of the others in the network. Recently, Huckfeldt, Sprague, and Johnson (2004) show that someone's influence on another person's vote choice is limited or augmented by the other viewpoints in the network. They term the relational characteristics of network influence as autoregressive influence. This research shows that impact of knowledge in social networks is also autoregressive.

I apply this autoregressive theory to investigate the influence of social network knowledge on vote choice. To examine this test, I create a measure of residual network knowledge, which is the average knowledge of the other network members. I hypothesize that the likelihood of voting for the same candidate for president in the United States' 2000 election—henceforth "vote similarity"—raises with the discussant's knowledge, but that residual network knowledge negatively affects dyadic vote similarity. I examine data from the 2000 American National Election Study (NES) because unique questions asked that year provide rich social network data to test. I find that vote similarity increases by five percentage points (with a standard error of two percentage points) with each level of perceived discussant political knowledge, while controlling for the residual political knowledge and preferences of the network, homogeneity between the discussant and the respondent, frequency of political discussion, education, partisanship, mobilization, ideology, and political interest. But vote similarity decreases by ten percentage points for each level of residual network knowledge, while controlling for these same factors.

Discovering this relationship is important because it may explain political knowledge influence in social networks. Taber (2003) states that the dilemma of how democracy can survive with so many politically incompetent dysfunctional citizens is one of the most important questions in political behavior research. He posits that political knowledge in social networks may offer the answer through what he terms "compositional aggregation" (Taber 2003, 458). In this process, "ordinary citizens contribute bits and pieces of information, preferences, and questions to the public discourse; the complex system puts things together" (Taber 2003, 458). He also states that this process needs a more thorough investigation. Much recent literature concerns the negative impact of low-information voting (e.g., Achen and Bartels 2004; Althaus 1998; Bartels 1996, 2005; Alvarez 1998; Delli Caprini and Keeter 1996). How do citizens with little political knowledge make vote choices? Some scholars posit that there are cues, heuristics, or other mechanisms that allow voters to take shortcuts (e.g., Lau and Redlawsk 1997; Page and Shapiro 1992; Popkin 1991; Sniderman, Brady, and Tetlock 1991). Bartels (1996) shows that these theories do not account for the difference between the informed and non-informed, and briefly mentions the influence of opinion leaders without testing their impact. Opinion leaders may influence vote choice through recommendations (Katz and Lazarsfeld 1955). Good recommendations enable low-information voters to make reasonable choices (Neuman 1986). To confirm the compositional aggregation theory, it is important to determine if voters are blindly following these leaders or if they consider other opinions. Social network influence is problematic for democracy if voters are influenced through mechanisms that lead to unthinking agreement. This research shows that voters are influenced by those they perceive to be knowledgable, but that they also are influenced by the other knowledgeable people they know. This signifies that social networking can help low-information voters, as networks provide information aggregated as group.

Opinion Leaders

Scholarship has long considered informal social networking as crucial to explain behavior (Lau and Ng 2001). For example, early studies found that neighbors often recommend products to each other (e.g., Whyte 1954). Sophisticated empirical research shows the impact of word-of-mouth (WOM) on a vast array of behavior (e.g., Brown and Reingen 1987; Coleman, Katz and Menzel 1957; Rogers 1962; Sheth 1971; Venkatraman 1989). A key development in WOM research was the development of the two-step hypothesis, which posits that opinion leaders learn about innovative products, candidates, and policies and then they introduce their network (Katz and Lazarsfeld 1955). While these opinion leaders tend to proselytize about products they enjoy, people often ask for their highly valued opinion (Cox 1963). The opinion leader's level of influence depends, in part, on how well they communicate. Vividly presented opinions have a larger impact than pallidly presented opinions (Heer, Kardes, and Kim 1991). Importantly, opinion leadership is also subjective, because they must only be perceived as knowledgeable (Silverman 1997). Opinion leaders may not actually know much about the products they endorse, but the more their networks believe they are knowledgeable, the more influential their advice. Thus, testing whether or not voters consider multiple opinions is an important test.

The opinion leader theory, however, does not consider relational autoregressive network characteristics. It states that knowledgeable people give advice to the less knowledgeable, but it does not consider the change in impact due to the difference in knowledge between network members (e.g., Neuman 1986). This is unfortunate because one of the original points of Katz and Lazarsfeld (1955, 105) was determining the most influential people in decision making. Modern research, however, has ignored this component. Huckfeldt, Johnson, and Sprague's (2004) recent development of the autoregressive theory demonstrates an appropriate methodology to test the hypothesis using network batteries. To test the hypothesis, I need to control for the residual knowledge of the other network members.

Social networks may explain distribution of vote choice information. Lau (2003) reviews the vast literature on behavioral decision making and states that "decision makers are generally guided by two competing goals (1) the desire to make a good decision; and (2) the desire to reach a decision with minimal cognitive effort" (Lau 2003, 32). He also states that this decision process applies to voting behavior. In the case of goal (2) an obvious strategy is to ask someone for help with the decision. But, because the decision maker also wants to make the correct decision—goal (1)—they will likely take the advice of a friend they perceive to be knowledgeable about the subject. The influence from opinion leaders may also depend on the relational level of knowledge of the other network members. Simply put, the more knowledge the rest of the network has, the less likely the influence from one member. Thus, I hypothesize that vote similarity increases as the level of perceived knowledge of the discussant increases, but decreases as the residual network knowledge raises. This research proceeds as follows. First, I discuss the relationship of social networks and vote choice. Then I review the data sources and methods of analysis. I then determine what influences vote similarity in social networks and conclude by discussing the results.

My hypothesis applies the autoregressive theory to opinion leader theory. In testing the hypothesis, I also control for these other suggested causes of vote choice similarity: network homogeneity, the autoregressiveness of political preferences, and opinion leadership. The contribution of this research is that it tests a theory of influence within networks that was heretofore ignored.

Data and Methods

I test the impact of social networks using again the NES data from 2000.

Social Network Variable Coding

In 2000, the NES collected network data by asking the respondents about the people within their social network. The NES asked the respondent to describe characteristics of the people with whom the respondent most often has political discussions. This process is called a name generator. There are two common critiques of name-generator data, one that it is not objective data on the discussant, and more specifically that these subjective interpretations—for example, of knowledge—are based on peripheral route persuasion. Firstly, although these are not objective data on the discussant's vote choice, it is important to test the hypothesis using the respondent's beliefs. The hypothesis is that networking changes people's beliefs about which candidate to vote for, based on receiving advice. Thus, what is important for this hypothesis is what the respondent believes (not necessarily knows) about their discussants. Secondly, psychologists refer to persuasion based on eloquence or physical attractiveness as "peripheral route persuasion" (Petty, Cacioppo, and Schumann 1983). Unfortunately, the data does not have information on physical, emotional, or other non-reason-based attributes that allow people to be viewed as intelligent and be persuasive. It is possible some discussants use this peripheral route to influence others, and that their influence is not based on real political knowledge. Huckfeldt, Sprague, and Levine (2000), however, use snowball surveys (where the respondents and their network members are surveyed) to obtain objective data on the accuracy of the respondents' interpretations of their discussants' characteristics (see also Ikeda and Huckfeldt 2001). They show that most people are able to accurately describe their discussants in name-generator surveys. Based on these empirical findings of validity, many researchers use name generators to investigate social networks (see Huckfeldt, Johnson, and Sprague 2004, 36). The dependent variable for dyadic agreement is Vote similarity for president in 2000, coded one if the respondent voted for the same candidate as their discussant and zero if not.

The key causal variables are created from the perceived level of political knowledge. The respondent rated the knowledge of each network member from not much (zero), average (one), and a great deal (two). Table 4.1 shows the distribution of knowledge for the discussants. Note: Cells are the percent of (total number in parenthesis) respondents who believe that their discussant knows either not much, average, or a great deal about politics from NES 2000. Percentages may not sum due to rounding. The discussants are described as having on average a little above average knowledge. The description given in the name generator allows me to create the Discussant's knowledge variable to test the opinion leader theory, which implies a positive influence. To test the autoregressive hypothesis, I create the Residual network knowledge measure by averaging the knowledge of the other network discussants. If people are actually considering multiple opinions based on political knowledge levels, high level of residual knowledge should more often lead to agreement with others than the dyad, i.e., I expect a negative influence on vote similarity. Thus, if a network has four discussants, I average the knowledge of the other three, and then repeat this process for every member in the group. This allows me to test the autoregressive impact of the residual knowledge of the others in the network. Two hundred ninety respondents list only one discussant. In these cases the network average is, of course, zero. In cases, where there are two or three discussants, the residual knowledge is averaged with the same procedure as with four-person networks.

Table 4.1: Respondent's Belief About Their Discussants' Level of Political Knowledge

Discussant	Not Much	Average	A Great Deal	Mean	Total
First	9.1 (104)	48.8 (557)	42.3 (483)	1.33	1141
Second	11.0 (94)	55.7 (478)	33.3 (285)	1.22	857
Third	12.6 (69)	53.2 (292)	34.1 (187)	1.21	548
Fourth	12.8 (42)	54.1 (177)	33.1 (108)	1.20	327

The impact of social networks is also determined by characteristics of the receiver of the information, the sender, and the network context. I use the combined perceived vote similarity of the other network members to measure Residual network agreement, as created by Huckfeldt, Johnson, and Sprague (2004, pp. 46-67). To create this variable, I sum the number of other members that vote for the same candidate as the respondent. Also, the more the dyad discusses politics, the more likely they will vote similarly, as this is a measure of in-group density which research shows congeals political attitudes (Huckfeldt, Ikeda, and Pappi 2005). How often each member discusses politics is coded from never (zero), rarely (one), sometimes (two), to often (three). Homophily between the respondent and the discussant may also lead to acceptance of advice. I measure the discussant's similarity to the respondent by including two measures of homogeneity. I use a measure that asks if the discussant goes to the Same church as the respondent because religion is a large determinant of vote choice in America. Additionally, I include a measure of whether the discussant is a Relative. Unfortunately, the NES does not have data on the discussant's race, an obvious limitation.

Control Variables

It is possible that persuasion from the respondent is influencing vote similarity. Thus, below I report two models: one with network characteristics and one including determinants from the respondents. Including the respondent's characteristics controls for the potentiality that the respondent is the opinion leader. First I include a measure that asks if the respondent thinks they are Better informed about politics and government than most people, coded from agree strongly (four), agree somewhat (three), neither agree nor disagree (two), disagree somewhat (one), disagree strongly (zero). I also include a measure that asks whether or not the respondent tried to Advocate why people should vote for or against one of the parties or candidates. The more Education (in years of schooling) the respondent has, the more stable their political choices and the more likely they may influence others. Partisanship is a well-known predictor of vote choice, and the more attached people are to their party, the less likely to take advice. Partisanship is measured from no preference (zero), independent but closer to one party (one), not very strongly partisan (two), and strongly partisan (three). Also mobilization simplifies vote choice and, thus, makes it easier to give advice. Mobilization is measured with a question that asks whether or not the respondent was contacted by a political party. Additionally, ideology may affect the willingness to give advice, as the more ideological have more intense political views. Ideology is measured from middle of the road (zero), slightly ideological (one), ideological (two), to extremely ideological (three). Interest in politics also may make someone more likely to give advice, and here is measured by whether the respondent is not much (zero), somewhat, (one), or very much (two) interested in politics.

Methods

As the data is clustered in groups of discussants, I follow Huckfeldt, Johnson, and Sprague (2004, p. 55) and correct the standard errors for clustering (see Rogers 1993). As Vote similarity is binary, I use a logistic regression model. In addition, I check for endogeneity between the dependent and causal variable because thinking someone is knowledgeable about politics may be due to vote similarity. You may think that your friend is smart because they vote the same way you do. For example, if you are Republican, and the discussant is a Republican, you may view them as more knowledgeable than your Democratic friend, simply due to political agreement. If the dependent variable is continuous, I can use the familiar two-stage least squares estimator to determine the impact of endogeneity. Here, I use the "ivprob" package for Stata to create an Amemiya generalized least squares (AGLS) model of endogeneity with a dichotomous dependent variable. Also, I create simulations from Clarify, drawn from the data to show the effect of a change in a quantity of interest on the dependent variable and calculate the predicted probabilities listed below.

Results

Receiver operator characteristic (ROC) plots show the goodness of fit of logistic regression models. The ROC plot shows the number of correctly predicted ones and zeroes. The ROC analysis shows that model 1 and model 2 in table 4.2 are successfully predicting a high percentage of the binary outcomes, as the curves are significantly above the forty-five-degree line of random chance. The indistinguishable lines overlap, thus showing that the respondent's characteristics do not add much to the predictive power of the model. Model 1 explains 69 percent of the variance of the dependent variable, while model 2 explains 71 percent.

The results in table 4.2 show that even after you control for the influence of other network members' political knowledge, the knowledge of the discussant has a positive effect on vote similarity. This impact is shown in models with and without the respondent's characteristics included. The chance of voting similarly increases by five percentage points (with a standard error of two percentage points) for each level of discussant knowledge. This confirms the opinion leader theory. Residual network knowledge, however, decreases vote similarity by ten percentage points (with a standard error of two percentage points) for each level of average residual knowledge. Thus, as predicted, the impact of information in social networks is autoregressive. The more knowledge the rest of the network has, the less likely a dyad will vote similarly. As shown by Huckfeldt, Johnson and Sprague (2004), more Residual network agreement increases the chance of voting for the same candidate by ten percentage points (with a standard error of one and half percentage points) for each network member voting similarly. The more often you speak about politics with someone, the more likely you vote for the same candidate, by about seven percentage points (with a standard error of two percentage points) for each level of frequency of discussion. If someone is a Relative you are more likely to vote similarly to them. The chance of relatives voting similarly is twelve percentage points (with a standard error of two percentage points) higher than non-relatives. Going to the Same church increases the likelihood of voting for the same candidate, but when the respondent's characteristics are added to the model, it is no longer significant. All four theories of network influence are verified by these results. In sum, the data shows that social networking has a strong impact on vote similarity.

Chapter Four

Table 4.2: Similarity of Vote Choice for the 2000 U.S. Presidential Election

Variable	1	(S. E.)	2	(S. E .)
Discussant's knowledge	0.178*	(0.078)	0.260***	(0.081)
Residual net. knowledge	-0.390**	(0.142)	-0.525***	(0.141)
Residual net agreement	0.613***	(0.069)	0.512***	(0.070)
Often	0.468***	(0.076)	0.391***	(0.075)
Relative	0.468***	(0.076)	0.503*	(0.099)
Same church	0.305	(0.202)	0.293	(0.182)
Interest			0.303***	(0.081)
Education	-		0.015	(0.012)
Ideology			0.185***	(0.052)
Party ID			0.191***	(0.049)
Mobilization			0.227*	(0.093)
Advocate	-		0.190*	(0.096)
Better in-formed			0.085*	(0.042)
Intercept	-1.492***	(0.178)	-2.190***	(0.270)
Number of cases	2761		2268	
Wald ^2	72.94***		269.71***	
-2 Log likelihood	-3661.07		-1364.13	

Note: Cells represent unstandardized coefficients and standard errors of logistic regression models for determinants of the respondent voting for the same candidate as their discussant. Standard errors corrected for clustering. Data is weighted from the 2000 NES.

The non-network variables also show a strong influence on the dyadic agreement. How better informed the respondent feels they are leads to a two-percentage-point increase for each level. Somewhat strangely, if the respondent was an advocate for a candidate or party, it leads to a four-percentage-point drop in vote similarity. It is possible that when advocating their vote choice, the respondent learned clearly of disagreement between them and their discussant, and that this increased clarity produces the drop in perceived agreement. Partisanship positively influences the likelihood of vote similarity. Interest, Mobilization, and Ideology also show a strong positive influence on vote similarity. Interestingly, the respondent's Education does not have an impact.

It is also interesting to see if this impact has partisan characteristics. In other words, perhaps Democrats or Republicans are more influenced by their social networks. To test this possibility, I split the data into discussants who are Bush voters and Gore voters. I ran the model with the same control variables as before. Figure 4.1 shows that there is no partisan effect, as the impact is almost the same for both groups of voters.

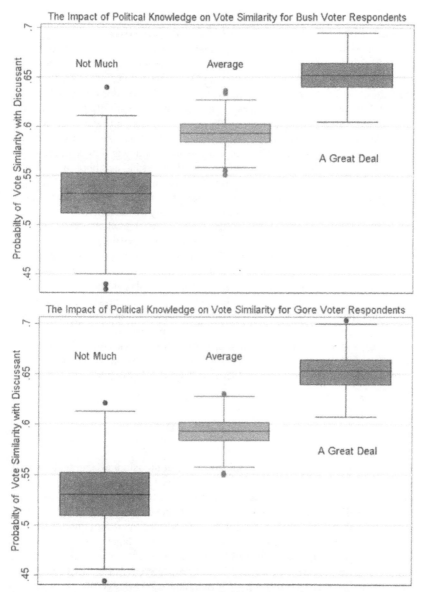

Figure 4.1: These graphs show that knowledgeable discussants have more vote similarity. The boxes represent the 95 percent confidence intervals for the predicted probability of a logistic regression model of vote similarity for Gore and Bush voters, while holding all else constant created by Clarify (King, Tomz, and Wittenberg 2000). Calculated from the model in table 4.2.

AGLS Regression Model Of Vote Similarity

To determine if the level of knowledge that the respondent assigns each discussant is influenced by whether or not they agree on politics, I create an AGLS regression model. Levine (2005, 135) uses the demographics of the discussant as an instrument to determine endogeneity in vote similarity. For the AGLS model, I follow Levine (2005, 135) in creating an instrumental variable from characteristics of the discussant. I use three characteristics that influence the level of knowledge of the discussant, but not vote similarity. I use the discussant's gender and whether or not the discussant is a coworker or a neighbor as instruments. Discussant male, Discussant coworker, and Discussant neighbor are dummy variables. These variables have a powerful influence on perceived Discussant knowledge, but have no impact on whether or not they vote similarly. Thus, these are intuitive instruments that should isolate any bi-causality.

In the AGLS model results, the Discussant's knowledge strongly positively influences vote agreement. The larger positive coefficient may be due to some imprecision in the instrument. Thus, we must be cautious in interpreting this model, but the results suggest that there is not a bi-causal relationship. The AGLS results show similar effects for all other variables as the models in table 4.2. The robustness of the results demonstrates that discussant knowledge is influential after controlling for the homophily effects on the assessment discussant's knowledge. This makes intuitive sense if people are not selective about whom they discuss politics with, and are not choosing discussants based on political criteria. People probably discuss politics with those that happen to be around them, and do not judge their discussant's knowledge by ideological agreement.

Conclusion

This research elucidates the mechanisms of the compositional aggregation theory and suggests that the concerns of social influence in vote by mail elections are unwarranted. In fact, if there is social influence it will come from informed members, and also be checked and balanced by the others of the social network. Citizens embedded in networks seem to consider multiple opinions when making vote choices. I find that social networks have a large influence on vote choice. In particular, the discussant's knowledge affects vote choice in a way similar to the autoregressive effect of political preferences found by Huckfeldt, Johnson, and Sprague (2004). As the discussant's knowledge increases there is greater likelihood of vote similarity, even after holding the other network members' knowledge constant. However, the significant negative impact of Residual network knowledge shows that the discussant's influence is limited by the knowledge of the others in the network. The opinion leader theory needs a modification to include the relational knowledge levels of others in the network. Future research should consider autoregressiveness when examining social network influence on other areas of political life, such as participation and policy support. This research also shows that the other two theories of network influence also affect vote similarity as predicted. The autoregressive influence of network political preference was replicated in this study. In addition, I find that homogeneity between the discussant and the respondent positively influences vote choice.

Table 4.3: Similarity of Vote Choice for the 2000 U.S. Presidential Election

Variable	Coef.	(S. E.)
Discussant's knowledge	0.644*	(0.322)
Residual network knowledge	-0.429***	(0.107)
Residual network agreement	0.331	(0.037)
Often	0.098	(0.103)
Relative	0.321***	(0.062)
Same church	0.236*	(0.112)
Interest	0.206***	(0.050)
Education	-0.001	(0.005)
Ideology	0.100**	(0.033)
Party identification	0.127***	(0.032)
Mobilization	0.129*	(0.058)
Intercept	-1.738***	(0.247)
Number of cases	2761	
Chi^2	320.80***	
-2 Log likelihood	-1371.12	

Table 4.3: Cells represent unstandardized coefficients and standard errors of an AGLS regression model for determinants of the respondent voting for the same candidate as their discussant. Discussant male, Discussant coworker, and Discussant neighbor are used as instruments on Discussant knowledge. Standard errors corrected for clustering. Data is weighted from the 2000 NES.

Chapter 5
Policy Opinions and Discussion Networks[*]

Continuing this reseach path, I now examine how people form policy preferences in social networks. Due to direct democracy's growing popularity, it matters directly for vote-by-mail systems how people form their opinions on policy, because voters vote directly on policies. If the vote-by-mail system allows more deliberative considerations of policies, it will inform us of how citizens choose in direct democracy in mail-ballot systems. A large literature stresses the non-rational nature of decision-making (see Lau 2003) for a recent review). Rational policy preferences require learning specific details in a competitive political environment. In most contentious policy debates, the choices are blurred through intense and creative marketing of policy outcomes. The emotionality of policy debates has prompted some researchers to doubt how rational people are when deciding which policies to support (e.g., Bartels 2005). This doubt is augmented because many people are unaware of policy choices or outcomes. Yet, some policies do provoke political responses, such as gay marriage referenda in the 2004 United States elections (McDonald 2004). The influence of social networks on many aspects of political behavior is well known, and may explain how policy choices can be made rationally by the average public. Yet, social network influence on policy preference has been ignored. This research tests the impact from social networking on policy preference. The potential impact of social networks is vastly increased if networks influence the policy preferences which in turn influence vote choice. Thus, discovering this effect may also inform our understanding of the stability of voting behavior.

*This chapter was co-authored with Ken'ichi Ikeda.

49

   I investigate the influence on policy preference by testing whether the likelihood of supporting a policy increases when one's social network members support a political party or candidate that also supports the policy. I examine policies asked in the NES: spending vs. service, the death penalty, abortion, equal rights, adoption by homosexuals, and school vouchers. I find that for these policies, the political beliefs of the network has a large impact on the respondent's beliefs, while controlling for the political knowledge of the respondent, network heterogeneity and size, partisanship, ideology, socioeconomic status, and policy-specific determinants.

   Discovering this relationship is important because it may explain how people with little political knowledge form policy opinions. If policy advice comes from opinion leaders in social networks, then there may be little problem for democracy because low-information voters will support similar policies as they would if they were knowledgeable. This makes the assumption that knowledgable and unknowledgeable members of close-knit social groups have the same political goals. We leave confirmation of this assumption to other researchers. This research shows that voters are influenced by their networks, and, thus, it may explain how low-information voters vote similarly to the more informed.

   The literature provides clear evidence of the power of social networks to affect voting and political participation, but it sheds little light on policy opinion formation. Perhaps different policies are more influenceable by networks. Further, policy is far more difficult to decipher than candidates whose personality, looks, and campaign marketing all help voters choose. The contribution of this research is that it tests network influence in an area of political behavior—policy preference—that was heretofore ignored.

Data

The data again come from the 2000 NES.

Social Network Variables

I create a variable that sums the perceived vote choice for each network member—up to four discussants are in each network—weighted by the amount of discussion from that member—coded from zero for no discussion, one for sometimes, and two for often. A separate effect from the information received in the network is the impact of homogeneity. Knowing diverse people may make one more willing to accept diverse opinions, which is a separate effect from the political advice received in networks. For example, if encounters with heterogeneity produce tolerance—as some literature shows (e.g., Sniderman, Brody, and Tetlock 1991)—then we must control for this second experiential impact from networking on policy beliefs. I measure network heterogeneity by coding networks by percentage of liberal or conservative parties. I then "fold" these data to make networks with 50 percent from each party equal zero, and the remaining networks are coded as the absolute distance from 50 percent. Thus, higher is more homogenous. I also control *Number of discussants* to ensure that doing more networking is also not altering policy beliefs.

Dependent variables

The policies are commonly discussed issues, which were asked on the NES. It is important to use these famous issues, because a high percentage of respondents will have an opinion about them. Each respondent was asked about the following policies:

Abortion There has been some discussion about abortion during recent years. I am going to read you a short list of opinions. Please tell me which one of the opinions best agrees with your view? You can just tell me the number of the opinion you choose. (1) by law, abortion should never be permitted. (2) the law should permit abortion only in case of rape, incest, or when the woman's life is in danger. (3) the law should permit abortion for reasons other than rape, incest, or danger to the woman's life, but only after the need for the abortion has been clearly established. (4) by law, a woman should always be able to obtain an abortion as a matter of personal choice. (7) other (specify) [vol] (8) dk

Spending vs. Service Some people think the government should provide fewer services even in areas such as health and education in order to reduce spending. Suppose these people are at one end of a scale, at point 1. Other people feel it is important for the government to provide many more services even if it means an increase in spending. Suppose these people are at the other end, at point 7. And, of course, some other people have opinions somewhere in between, at points 2, 3, 4, 5, or 6.

Equal Rights Our society should do whatever is necessary to make sure that everyone has an equal opportunity to succeed. Do you agree strongly, agree somewhat, neither agree nor disagree, disagree somewhat, or disagree strongly with this statement?

Death Penalty Do you favor or oppose the death penalty for persons convicted of murder?

Adoption by Homosexuals Do you think gay or lesbian couples, in other words, homosexual couples, should be legally permitted to adopt children?

School Vouchers Do you favor or oppose a school voucher program that would allow parents to use tax funds to send their children to the school of their choice, even if it were a private school?

Control variables

I must control for other factors that influence policy beliefs. Chiefly, *Ideology* affects policy beliefs. *Ideology* is coded from zero to four with conservative higher. Party identification is coded one for Democratic Party and zero for all others. Socioeconomic factors affect policy, and unless controlled can bias the results. Race is a determinant of policy, which we control for with *Whites* coded as one, and others zero. *Hispanics* are coded one, and others zero. The other demographics that influence policy preference are being *Male*, *Age* measured in years, *Education* in years, and *Income* coded ordinally in 5,000-dollar categories. Knowledge of politics is an important determinant of policy preference (Alvarez 1998; Delli, Caprini, and Keeter 1996). The more knowledgable the respondent is the more stable their political choices and the less likely they may be influenced by others. As used by Bartels (1996, p. 203), we include the survey interviewer's assessment of the respondent's political *Knowledge*, coded from one for not knowledgeable to five for very knowledgeable about politics.

Some variables are only used with some models, as they would be inapplicable for some policies. Thus, *Religious* and *Born again* are dichotomous variables that measure these characteristics—coded one if so, and zero if not— and used in models for *Abortion* and *Homosexual adoption*. Media usage is controlled for in models for *Spending vs. service* and *Death penalty*. *Media* is measured by a question that asks whether or not the respondent watches television programs about politics. Trust also has been shown to influence certain policy beliefs (Hetherington 1998). *Trust* is coded one if the respondent feels people are trustworthy, and zero if not.

The Impact of Networks on Policy Preference

I ran separate logistic regression models for each of the dependent varaibles. The results show that the level network Gore support has an effect on every policy considered. *Spending vs. Service, Death Penalty, Abortion, Equal Rights, Gay Rights,* and *School Vouchers* all show strong significant effects.

The more Gore voters in your social network, the more you support liberal polices, holding all else constant. The models shown fit the data well, and many of the covariates are statistically significant at the $p < .05$ level. The significant variables match their predictions in all models. In Figure 5.1, I show that predicted probability of supporting the policy when the respondent has either four Republican friends or four Democratic friends, while holding all else constant. This graph was created by Clarify and the kernel density plots represent the 95 percent confidence intervals for the predicted probability of a logistic regression model of policy support, while holding all else constant. Thus substantive impact of discussion networks on policy preferences is large, suggesting that the open deliberative process used in voting-by-mail systems will be impactful on decision-making for ballot measures.

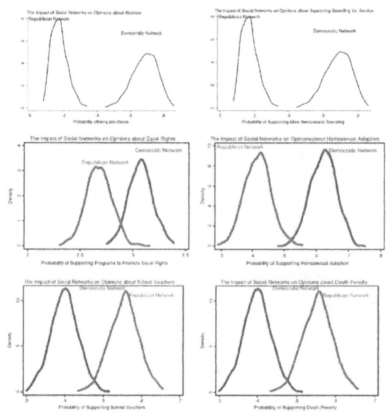

Figure 5.1: These graphs show that discussants influence public policy preferences.

Conclusion

This research finds that political discussions in social network help citizens form policy preferences. This suggests the more deliberative vote-by-mail system will also help voters choose on referenda and initiative questions, which are related to public policy. Theories on the need for political discussion for a successful democracy are linked to a long philosophical tradition that stretches from Habermas in the twentieth century back to Rousseau, and even Aristotle. These theorists stress that being a political animal means that we need to use political discussion to resolve our differences. For example, Habermas argues for constitutional reforms to create structures that permit and encourage political discussion to allow citizens to learn about politics from their peers. The research supports this, and more reforms that promote political discussion should be considered and implemented.

That policy preference was shown to be influenced by political discussion has interesting possibilities for democratic theory. This research shows our opinions on politics is a product of communication in informal networks. other studies show that interpersonal communication is sometimes necessary to comprehend the nightly news (e.g., Robinson and Levy 1986). Thus, our political understanding often derives from informal networks, even if the original information comes from mass media. In this sense, without support from networks, our political comprehension may be limited. This is important because understanding the influence of social networks may allow opportunities to develop programs to increase political knowledge. For example, one suggestion is for government to promote political understanding by sponsoring intergroup interaction (Ackerman and Fishkin 2004; Leib 2004). If programs can be created that sponsor political discussion, they may force people to encounter new ideas and have a large positive impact on policy preference.

One caveat is that we have no data on whether advice is offered, although the model does contain data on the amount of discussion. The results are, hence, limited to conclusions based on the assumption that advice was given during the political discussions, and this is what lead to the similarity of policy preference. This is an area future research should examine when considering who is influential in social networks.

Chapter 6
Rational Patriotism and Social Networking

What is the relationship between patriotism, rationality, and social networking? So far we have seen that exposure to diverse viewpoints in discussion networks leads to greater rational choices. I want to extend this to a difficult area for rationality: patriotism. Patriotism is often associated with irrationality (Kateb 2006). But recent research political psychology has shown a link between a certain type of rational patriotism and social networking (Schatz, Staub, and Lavine, 1999). These researchers posit that the causal arrow flows from patriotism to social networking, but a counter perspective in the social capital literature assumes that causation runs in the opposite direction, from social networking to patriotism. Opposite of the political psychology literature on patriotism, it is often suggested by social capital theorists that greater social networking leads to more patriotism. I seek to untangle these relationships by positing a bi-causal relationship between these beliefs and actions.

I use a Structural Equation Model (SEM) to empirically establish the recursive causal relationship between patriotism and social networking. To do so, I also consider new research in political psychology which shows that there are two dimensions of patriotism based of love of country and how that relates with criticism of the country. New research shows that measures of criticism must be combined with measures of love of country to model the impact of patriotism correctly, which produces two patriotic dimensions (Huddy and Khatib, 2007, Davidov, 2009). Articulating the multiple patriotic dimensions allows us to test these recursive relationships with social networking. This research provides a fuller picture of the relationship of patriotism with social networking than has been provided previously in political theory or political psychology.

This research is important because critics of service learning, civic education, and other efforts to stimulate social networking often complain that doing so is type of propaganda that leads to nationalism (for a review of these criticisms, see Mitchell, 2008). They suggest that it is better for citizens to remain critical of the system, rather than be forced into social networking programs that reinforce blind patriotism (Pompa, 2005). A similar critique comes from political theory, which suggests that patriotism is generally negative, and efforts to promote it through participation are bad because citizens will lose their critical abilities with greater patriotism (see, e.g., Cohen and Nussbaum, 1996; MacIntyre, 1995; or Kateb, 2006). These critics, however, ignore modern research that shows that patriotism has a constructive critical style in addition to a blind patriotism.

For example, Schatz, Staub, and Lavine (1999) show that patriotism has two dimensions, with an oft-ignored constructive patriotism dimension which influences social networking. Constructive patriots may at times be angry with and ashamed by America's actions, but they still love their country. These constructive patriots generally have traits that are healthy for democracy, and correlate with greater social networking. Constructive patriots must be distinguished from blind patriots who show an uncritical love of their nation. Blind patriots are never or rarely ashamed of/angry at the United States, and were found to have less social networking in the past. While Schatz, Staub, and Lavin's (1999) non-experimental study was based on as convenience sample of college students, Huddy and Khatib (2007) find similar results with a nationally representative sample (see also Sullivan, Fried, and Dietz 1992). While extremely interesting and path-breaking, this line of research did not account for potential endogeniety between social networking and patriotism, and so cannot answer the critiques of service learning and other stimulation programs. Thus, as more and more school systems use service learning, and towns are developing programs to stimulate social networking, it is crucial to test which type of patriotism is influenced by social networking, or whether patriotism is influenced at all by it.

Patriotism and Rationality in Political Theory

Political theorists view patriotism as a pathology. Indeed, MacIntyre famously described it as "a permanent source of moral danger" (MacIntyre 1995, p. 226). These arguments have an important cognitive component that is often overlooked or left unsaid. Nussbaum (1996), Kateb (2006) and others have waged war on the concept of loving one's country by confusing it with losing the ability to rationally analyze one's nation's actions. In fact, the entirety of MacIntyre's famous quote reveals a fundamental flaw in this line of thinking. Fully, he says that patriotism is "a permanent source of moral danger because of the way it places our ties to our nation beyond rational criticism" (MacIntyre 1995, p. 226). The underlying problem with their critique of patriotism is that it combines two distinct concepts. First, there is love of one's country. Separately, there is the ability or inclination for rational criticism, to be able to negatively judge one's country when it makes mistakes.

Perhaps these critics believe these separate concepts are so empirically correlated or causally related that it is useful to speak of them in the same breath. Research shows they are not, and unpacking these concepts reveals a worthwhile extension to our theoretical understanding of patriotism. For example, using survey data from twenty three nations, Davidov (2009) shows that constructive patriotism can be distinguished from nationalistic patriots by their ability to be critical of their country. Unpacking these concepts allows us to show below that a majority of Americans love their country and are also ashamed of it sometimes. Thus, the mere presence of love does not negate the cognitive abilities of these citizens. Testing the cognitive limitations caused by patriotism reveals that much of the concern is unwarranted.

One may ask, even if patriotism can sometimes not lead to blind obedience, what actual value does it have? This is an important pedagogical question, because civic education often involves patriotic symbology. One common answer is that constructive patriotism provides enough affection that we will toil to correct our nation's problems. For example, in his first inaugural address, Barack Obama states "we must choose our better history" to inspire us to work diligently to improve America (Obama 2009a). Here, he is using patriotism as a motivating device. But it is crucial to note that by saying better history, it is crystal clear that America has a worse history. Obama's style of patriotism does not negate the ability to be ashamed of its mistakes. Yet, this style of patriotism still inspires us to not defect in our daily national prisoner's dilemma. Without affection, what drives the motivation to be involved in fixing the country's problems by undertaking the requirements to understand the pressing issues? We know that rational ignorance does not benefit the society, only the individual shirkers (Nie, Verba, and Petrocik 1976). Some scholars—often called civic nationalists—stress that it is crucial to find inspiring national myths to motivate the rationally ignorant to not freeload (see Abizadeh 2004). But there is nothing mythical about stating that America has better and worse histories, it is rather a clearheaded analytical appraisal of its past. After making this rational cleavage between better and worse, one can then become emotionally attached to the better history. Rationality and emotional bonds are therefore not mutually exclusive. Thus, Obama's style of patriotism has the advantage of facilitating both the emotional bonds that civic nationalists say are needed to solve large problems, while still allowing the critical analysis required by government by the people.

One exception in political theory is Viroli (1995), who conducted a major recent study that also separates patriotism from nationalism. Particularly he finds that people have used patriotism for centuries to achieve goals and that it is commonly separated by these people from nationalism. He outlines a theoretical model, however, that is different from the concern over patriotic cognition examined here. His research does not focus on the perceived lack of critical capacity of patriots versus nationalists, but rather examines the difference in xenophobic beliefs in national supremacy that nationalists have and patriots do not. Basically, his theory suggests that love of country does not mean a necessary denigration of an out-group, or a claim of supremacy for the in-group. The history of civic republicanism, according to this research, shows that many have used the language of patriotism to achieve great national goals without using revanchism, as Obama did in the preceding example. Thus, the common fear of many political theorists that hatred is needed for motivating behavior is unfounded. The language of love of country can be used by motivators without reverting to attacking an enemy or stressing supremacy. This is a major breakthrough in political theory because it provides an eloquent analysis and evidence as to why patriotism is not xenophobic or supremacist (see also Muller 2007).

While the insights provided by Viroli (1995) may explain why patriots do not have to be xenophobic, it does not explain all possible distinctions between patriotism and nationalism. Prior empirical research deepens our understanding of patriotism by showing that patriots can be critical about the country they love (see Huddy and Khatib 2007). As blind support or critical analysis are known to highly predict behavior, the ability to critically analyze one's nation will likely influence public policy preferences. Blindly supporting the government will likely create a profound influence to support the polices of that government. Demonstrating the influence of patriotic cognition on public policy preferences increases our knowledge over the range of effects that patriotism can produce.

There is no denying, however, the existence of the type of people that Kateb, Nussbaum, and MacIntyre worry about. Indeed, one of the benefits of this research is quantifying their number in the population. The problem is with defining them as the only type of patriot, whereas research shows there are constructive patriots who can be critical (Schatz, Staub, and Lavine 1999). The people with nationalistic patriotic cognition values are people who can see no wrong with the United States. That implies two possible causes. First, they could be making the same mistake that the critics of patriotism are making, in that they may see any criticism as being exactly inversely proportional to love of country. Second, there is a long literature on manifest destiny and our civil religion (Bellah 1967). These people may have quasi-metaphysical belief in the divine blessing of America, which would imply national infallibility because God has divined this country's destiny. Thus the empirical literature offers a useful corrective to much of the theoretical literature on patriotism, as the cognitive abilities of constructive patriotism must be separated from nationalistic patriotism (Schatz, Staub, and Lavine 1999). But this does not fully address the potential for irrationality in the public, as there can be irrational dislike of one's country also, and this is missing from most empirical studies of patriotism in political psychology.

Patriotism in Political Psychology

The empirical literature up to this point has investigated patriotism and rationality in a few articles (e.g., Schatz, Staub, and Lavine 1999). The chief problem is that political psychology has not fully appreciated the importance of decision science on patriotism. Basically, the unsaid problem of nationalistic feelings or blind patriotism is that is deterministic, as it does not leave open the potential for error. Determinism will only be correct in the unlikely case that all of the important actions are either positive or negative. We know from decision science that most correct decision-making is probabilistic, which recognizes the inherent diversity in most things (Heitele 1975). In other words, the crucial question is not whether the United States is always right or always wrong, but rather it is how often is the United States is acting beneficially or not. The starting assumption should be that there have been good and bad, or correct and incorrect, actions. With topics as complex as the actions of the United States, it would be nearly impossible for the United States to have acted always negatively or positively, however defined, because the thousands of actions that the United States takes each year create too many possible decisions for all of them to be disagreeable or all agreeable with anyone. Probabilistic thinking is what is offered by Obama's constructive patriotism, because it fully acknowledges the possibility of both success and failure. A chief contribution of this article is to define and model two additional types of patriotic cognition systems, which are based on deterministically negative views of America.

Political psychology literature has not examined deterministic thinking in non-patriots. These people do not like anything about their country, and are quite different from the constructive patriots described in Huddy and Khatib (2007). These anti-Americanists are just as irrational as the nationalists because they do not leave open the possibility that America can do good. For example, Obama speaking about European anti-Americanism, but just as applicable in America, says "(i)nstead of recognizing the good that America so often does in the world, there have been times where (anti-Americanists) choose to blame America for much of what's bad" (Obama 2009b). Obama again states clearly the theme of America achieving both good and bad, but this time it is the anti-Americanists who are deterministically blaming the United States, and refusing to acknowledge benefit from America's actions. To fully understand the impact of patriotism, researchers should model these deterministically thinking anti-Americanists. Thus, the previous empirical models are misspecified because they ignore irrational anti-Americanists. In other words, what is important is an eternal vigilance over the nation's actions, and radicals who are always opposed to a nation make the same cognitive error as do nationalists. Thus, the prior research has not fully investigated the relationship of love of country and cognition. I seek to expand on these findings on the relationship between social networking and patriotism with a fuller theoretical model based on a counter

conception of the relationship between these variables in the social capital literature (discussed in depth below). To test the causal pathways of these relationships, I use a SEM of survey data from the 2004 American National Election
Studies (NES). I expect social networking to alter patriotism differentially, and
account for possible endogeniety. The findings show that constructive patriotism
promotes social networking, and that social networking separately increases
constructive patriotism. Conversely, I also find that blind patriotism lowers social networking, and that social networking lowers blind patriotism. These effects are robust to controlling for party identification, ideology, strength of partisanship, strength of ideology, interest, efficacy, political trust, and
socioeconomic demographics. These findings suggest that critics of service
learning and other stimulation programs are wrong about the impact of social
networking. Social networking has the opposite effect than what was feared, as
it actually promotes critical thinking about the country, as well as love for it.

This research proceeds as follows. First, I discuss the chief theoretical
and empirical work on social capital. I then differentiate the styles of patriotism
in the American public, and show how they may interact with social networking.
Then I review the data sources and codings. Next, I determine where the public
falls in this rubric, test the influence of these values, and conclude by discussing
the results.

Although Putnam (1993, 2000) does not provide a detailed analysis of
the relationship between patriotism and social networking, other researchers
have previously examined this issue in part. The civic culture literature mentions
this effect (e.g., Almond and Verba, 1963). By considering the political discussion and social networking literature, I show now how there should be more
constructive patriotism after working on social networking projects because it
facilitates a deeper understanding of and affect for the nation.

How Social Networking Alters Patriotism

Based on research on social capital discussed above, I develop a theoretical
model of how social networking alters patriotism. It consists of two widely validated claims over the impact of social networking. Firstly, a large literature
shows that face-to-face interaction and the communal spirit gained through participation engenders better feelings about society (see, e.g., Ikeda and Richey,
2009). In this view, social networking develops the inherent norms of reciprocity experienced when working together, which makes people feel that their
neighbors will treat them fairly (Rothstein, 2005). So, the first impact on patriotism from social networking will be an increase in care for the society that they
worked to help. The second impact of social networking on patriotism involves
developing knowledge about societal problems. It has been widely shown that
social networking increases knowledge of politics and society's problems (see
Galston, 2007 for a summary). In fact, many forms of social networking are

directed toward fixing societal problems. With the increase in experiential knowledge of America's problems gained through voluntary activities, social networking will develop critical citizens with a list of things they want changed about their nation.

We should then expect two things to flow from social networking: increased love and increased criticism for their society. Thus, social networking should increase constructive patriotism. These improved feelings toward others combined with improved knowledge of society's problems will develop a constructive patriotism that is loving and critical. At the same time, these enlightening experiences may also show that the nation is not always good or without problems, and contains hypocrisies. By greater social networking, people will encounter realities that bust the myths that undergird and motivate blind patriotism. These experiences will then directly work to lower blind patriotism, which is blind to the nation's problems. In sum, the theory predicts that social networking promotes constructive patriotism, and lessens blind patriotism. Based on these ideas I will investigate the possible endogenous relationship between social networking and these two types of patriotism.

The hypotheses are based on theories of the relationship between patriotism and social networking. I test whether the theory described above is correct, that social networking increases constructive patriotism and lowers blind patriotism. Hypothesis 1a: Social networking will increase constructive patriotism. Hypothesis 1b: Constructive patriotism will increase social networking. Hypothesis 2b: Social networking will decrease blind patriotism. Hypothesis 2a: Blind patriotism will decrease social networking. Now, let's examine the data I use to test these hypotheses.

Data

This research uses the 2004 NES data. These data were used because they are from the most recent survey that has the type of nuanced patriotism questions that are needed to test the theory. These questions were not asked in more recent iterations of the NES or other surveys such as the General Social Survey. The response rate was 66.1 percent, or 1,212 out of 1,833. Full information about the sampling procedure, question wordings, and survey methodology is available at the NES website

I follow other research on patriotism and use a scale of positive and negative questions on feelings toward the nation (Davidov 2009). The first question measures love of country by asking "How strong is your love for your country?" This is coded from extremely strong (3), very strong (2), somewhat strong (1), and not very strong (0). I also include a question that measures how the respondent answers "when you see the American flag flying does it make you feel, (3) Extremely good, (2) Very good, (1) Somewhat good, and (0) Not very good?" I also measure criticism of the country's actions, and if they view them as a mistake. Of course, for each individual these mistakes will be different, such as a pro-life person viewing legalized abortion as an abomination, or another person perhaps viewing the treatment of detainees as something to be ashamed of. Ashamed is measured by the level of agreement or disagreement with the statement "there are some things about America today that make me feel ashamed of America." This is coded from agree (2), neither agree nor disagree (1), or disagree (0). I also use an item that asks if there are some things about America today that make me feel angry about America. This is also coded from agree (2), neither agree nor disagree (1), or disagree (0).

Here, I expect both constructive and blind patriots to score highly on the love of country and flag questions. In the principal component analysis, both should load highly on these two affect questions, as both types are theoretically expected to love their country. Only the unpatriotic will score low on these questions. The differential between constructive and blind patriots comes from a willingness to critique the country, and is measured with the ashamed and angry questions. On these questions the blind patriots will score low and will load negatively in the principal component analysis, but the constructive patriots and the unpatriotic will score highly and load strongly. To measure both dimensions—which includes the unpatriotic at the opposite end of the dimensions—we need questions that measure both affect and the willingness to be critical.

I use these variables in a principal component analysis to show that there are in fact two dimensions for patriotism. I then use the two principal components from this analysis as variables in the SEM models. First, I show in table 6.1 the results of a principal component analysis which shows the bi-dimensionality of patriotism. Table 6.2 shows that there is a significant factor loading for those who either have affection and feel little shame or anger toward the United States. This matches the theorized blind dimension. There is also a separate significant factor that loads on both measures of affection and dissatisfaction, and this matches the theoretically predicted dimension of constructive patriotism. The test of independence rejects the null hypothesis at $p = 0.00000$, signifying a bi-dimensional relationship between these factors. Table 6.2 allows us to know how many in the population are in each category. The constructive dimension of patriotism explains 28.3 percent of the variance, and the blind patriotism dimension explains 49.3 percent. Thus, there is nearly twice as much blind patriotism than constructive patriotism in this sample. Both of these factors have significant eigenvalues well over 1.0. Although most of the respondents express some love of country, these eigenvalues well above 1.0 suggest that this enough variance to distinguish these factors. Thus, patriotism is bi-dimensional.

The measure of social networking sums respondent involvement in four actions, by asking the respondent if they have: 1. worked with other people to deal with some issue facing your community, 2. attended a meeting about an issue facing your community or schools, 3. telephoned, written a letter to, or visited a government official to express your views on a public issue; and 4. taken part in protest or march in last year. This measure has been used extensively (e.g., Tolbert, McNeal, and Smith 2003), and will serve as an accurate measure of social networking.

Table 6.1: Patriotic Values in the 2004 NES

	Blind	**Constructive**
Love	0.4701	0.5657
Flag	0.5306	0.4322
Ashamed	-0.4979	0.4987
Angry	-0.4996	0.4945
Eigenvalue	1.97268	1.13547
Proportion	0.4932	0.2839

Table 6.1: Cells represent principal components (eigenvectors) of a principal component analysis of the respondent's answers to questions about love of the United States, feelings about the American flag, and feelings of shame and anger about the United States. See text for details.

I must also control for other known causes of public opinion. Ideology and party identification often influence public opinion, and must be controlled in the models below. Ideology is measured on a seven-point scale, with conservative being higher. Party identification is measured on a seven-point scale with strongly attached to the Democratic Party to strongly attached to the Republican party. I also fold these two variables and create a measure of strength of ideology and strength of partisanship, where the most liberal or conservative or most partisan are ranked (3), the somewhat (2), a little (1) and nonideological or nonpartisan (0). As political trust is a key component of both social capital and patriotism, it may cause both variables and these results may be spurious. To alleviate these concerns, I include a political trust variable. The measure of political trust uses a standard question from the NES, by asking the respondent "How much of the time do you think you can trust the government in Washington to do what is right?" The answers are coded as just about always (3), most of the time (2), or only some of the time (1), never (0). Interest is an question noting how much interest respondents give politics or the election in 2004. Efficacy is a question of the respondents' feelings toward their ability to influence politics. Finally, socioeconomic demographics influence public opinion, and are entered into the models below. I control for being male, being Hispanic, being Black, income in $5,000 categories, years of education, years of residency, being immigrants, and age in years.

Methods

SEMs are often used in political science (e.g., Chang and Chu, 2006), and are quite well known with large established literatures explaining their use (see Bollen, 1989; Woodbridge, 2002, 256-270; Schumacker and Lomax, 2004). Thus, I need not delve too deep in explaining their intricacies, but I should note briefly why I chose this modeling strategy. It is entirely possible that the relationships examined here are endogenous. For example, being civically engaged may make someone patriotic, as they should care more about the country after working to improve it. But also likely is that patriotism will drive people to become civically engaged. These types of chicken-and-egg questions plague social science. Most researchers simply assume these problems are non existent, or, at most, use an instrumental variables approach on one of the regressors, such as a two-stage least squares model. The chief benefit of SEMs is that they allow for a far more plausible model of the gooey intertwined relationships that social scientists study. They provide an accurate assessment of the relationships of endogenous and exogenous regressors. Matching and other methods such as two-stage least squares are fine for when a researchers wants to establish better causal estimates of one endogenous regressor on another, but to determine the bi-causal impact of both at the same time, a SEM is superior.

Importantly, the model meets the Rank-Order conditions, which are necessary to ensure that the model is identified (Koopmans, 1949). The Rank-Order conditions are the necessary and sufficient conditions to interpret the SEM as a causal relationship without endogeniety. This is met because the number of exogenous parameters is greater than the number of endogenous ones (the order condition), and because the rank of the information matrix is equal to the number of free parameters in the model (the rank condition) (Joreskog and Sorbet, 1998). Thus, SEM is an appropriate modeling strategy for these relationships. The chief idea of these models is that the exogenous regressors provide leverage to use when analyzing the relationships of the endogenous regressors, similar to the more familiar two-stage least squares approach. When the Rank-Order conditions are met, we know that these exogenous regressors provide enough power to estimate the endogenous relationships.

Results

As for the four hypotheses on the impact on political behavior, 1a, 1b, 2a, and 2b are all confirmed by these data. Starting with the predictors of social networking, we see that constructive patriotism increased social networking, while there is statistically significant negative relationship between blind patriotism and social networking. This replicates the prior research, but also accounts for the endogenous relationship with social networking. Opting out of collective action is a well-understood problem for societies (Ostrom, 1998), and this sheds light on why blind patriots do not become active in their communities. It shows that constructive patriotism is a foundation to spark communal action. In the interest of space, the control variables are omitted from this discussion and table 16, but the results basically match prior literature. Substantively, if using standardized coefficients, we see that a one standard deviation increase in social networking creates about one half a standard deviation decrease in blind patriotism. Also, a one-standard-deviation increase in social networking increases constructive patriotism by half of a standard deviation. This shows that, at least for this sample, constructive patriotism is impacted by social networking at a about the same level as blind patriotism. I have no theoretical explanation for this equal substantive impact, and it is either a real effect based on how these beliefs interact with participation, or it may be a function of this time period or sample. Future work should examine this proportionate impact.

Now, let's examine the relationships of social networking with the two dimensions of patriotism. First we see that social networking causes people to have more constructive patriotism. Note that crucially this SEM removes the bicausal influence of patriotism on social networking.

Table 6.2: Structural Equation Model

Variable	Coef.	S. E.	
Equation 1 : Social networking			
Blind	-0.444***	(0.038)	
Constructive	1.010***	(0.119)	
Intercept	0.783***	(0.044)	
Obs.	851	chi2	161.55 ***
Equation 2 : Constructive patriotism			
Community participation	0.504***	(0.066)	
Intercept	-0.390***	(0.065)	
Obs.	851	chi2	58.74***
Equation 3 : Blind patriotism			
Community participation	-0.823***	(0.106)	
Intercept	0.644***	(0.101)	
Obs.	851	chi2	60.13***

Table 6.2: Cells represent unstandardized coefficients and standard errors of a SEM regression model for determinants of Blind patriotism, Constructive patriotism, and Community participation. The other endogenous variables used in the SEM were Party ID, Ideology, strength of partisanship, strength of ideology, Interest, Efficacy, National trust, and the exogenous variables were Residency, Religiosity, Parents were Immigrants, Male, Income, Education, Age, Hispanic, and Black. ***$p<.001$

These results show that helping your community teaches lessons in what Putnam (1993, pp. 89-90) called a school of democracy. Participants have more love of their nation after volunteering, but also are able to see its faults more clearly. The school of democracy teaches both the successes and problems, and that recognition of good and bad is exactly what distinguishes constructive patriots from blind patriots. This is interesting, because social networking causes many beneficial things for democratic society, and these results suggest that more work on the relationship of social capital and patriotism is needed. The influences of blind dimension of patriotism show that social networking has a significant negative relationship, which confirms my hypothesis. Social networking lessens the likelihood of ignoring societal problems. In the interest of space, the control variables are omitted from this discussion, but the results basically match prior literature. Substantively, a one-standard-deviation increase in blind patriotism, creates about one third a standard deviation decrease in social networking. Also, a one-standard-deviation increase in constructive patriotism increases social networking by one standard deviation. This shows that, at least for this sample, that constructive patriotism has much greater impact than blind patriotism. Again, I have no theoretical explanation for this larger substantive impact, but future researchers should examine this disproportionate impact.

All of the hypotheses are confirmed in the SEM. Most importantly, we see that social networking increases constructive patriotism and lessens blind patriotism, while these patriotism variables have similar impacts on social networking.

Conclusion

The findings show that the concern that service-learning or other programs that promote social networking are wrong to imply that greater participation leads to a loss of critical abilities and greater blind patriotism. This research shows that social networking has the opposite impact on the two dimensions of patriotism. Social networking was found to increase constructive patriotism, and lessen blind patriotism. I also find that relationships found in prior research hold in the SEM, which accounts for endogeneity. Constructive patriotism increases social networking, while blind patriotism lowers it. I show that an important causal distinction needs to be made about claims of patriotism's relationship with social networking. Future research should consider these endogenous relationships when studying how social networking interacts with patriotism. The results suggest that the stimulation of social networking would be beneficial for critical citizenship and should be promoted.

Research currently has not studied patriotism enough, and, more specifically, the relationship of social networking to patriotism needs far greater work. Specifically, pedagogical work on promoting social networking through service learning and how that may relate to constructive patriotism is worthwhile to investigate. Also, as social networking has been thought to be decreasing in the United States over the last fifty years (see Putnam, 2000), it may have impacted patriotism, which would possibly have eventual impacts on public opinion and vote choice. Future research should investigate these aspects of change over time.

Chapter 7
What Promotes Political Discussion and Advocacy?[*]

In the next two chapters, I examine the systematic influences on political discussion. What relationship do campaigns have with political advocacy? By "advocacy" I mean a specific type of political communication where an individual attempts to recommend their preferred candidate or campaign in discussion with another person. We know relatively little about how campaign activity influences this type of interpersonal communication. Political discussion research often focuses on general discussion, without analyzing interesting subsets of interpersonal communication, such as political advocacy. Advocating for a candidate is crucial to understand because this is where citizens make clear statements of their beliefs when trying to influence others (O'Keefe 2002), which is valuable in spreading information in discussion networks (Huckfeldt, Johnson, and Sprague 2004). I posit that greater campaign spending may create an excited environment that drives citizens to advocate for their preferred candidate. Vigorous campaigning has long been understood as a catalyst for citizen action in elections (Rosenstone and Hansen 1993). I anticipate that campaigns with greater resources will work as more powerful stimulants on the likelihood of advocating for a candidate. Greater campaign spending may enlist citizens into the campaign, thereby prompting citizens to speak on behalf of a candidate.

There is a large, growing literature on political discussion (Zuckerman 2005) that clearly shows that interpersonal communication has a profound influence on political behavior (Ryan 2010). Talking politics transfers important

1. This chapter was co-authored with J. Benjamin Taylor.

67

information (Eveland 2004; Gastil and Dillard 1999), motivates participation in politics (Klofstad 2007; McClurg 2006), influences vote choice (Huckfeldt, 2001), and promotes tolerance (Ikeda and Richey 2009). Past research on discussion also yields key network and individual factors that make discussion more likely (Huckfeldt and Sprague 1995). Missing from this research is an investigation of the macro-level determinants of not just discussion, but advocating for one's candidate. To help answer this question, I research the effect of campaigns on political advocacy. Specifically, I posit that increases in campaign spending will correlate with an increase in the likelihood of citizens advocating for a candidate, because spending creates exciting macro-environments that stimulate advocative interpersonal communication.

This research is important because many pundits and scholars worry over the influence of campaign spending in discouraging citizen involvement in politics. Campaign spending is thought to depress enthusiasm for politics, primarily through negative advertising (Ansolabehere, Iyengar, and Simon 1994; Ansolabehere and Iyengar 1996). I know, however, that campaigns generally distribute information that helps lower the costs of participating (Downs 1957), and bring people into politics through mobilization (Rosenstone and Hansen 1993). The ability of campaigns to engage in mobilization and spread campaign information should be greater with increased spending. Recent research also shows that even negative campaigns have benefits for politics, such as higher quantities of issue-specific charges and generating public engagement (Geer 2006). Also, negative campaigns might encourage learning by promoting information searches (Brader 2006). Based on these findings of the positive influence of campaigns on citizens' engagement, I investigate whether campaign spending encourages citizens to advocate on behalf of a candidate.

I test whether greater levels of campaign spending correlate with an increase in this special type of interpersonal communication about politics. Using multilevel logistic regression models of American National Election Studies (NES) data from presidential elections from 1976 to 2008, I find that greater campaign spending correlates with greater political advocacy. I also find that the likelihood of being an advocate correlates with greater political discussion, television usage, interest in politics, partisanship, efficacy, and socioeconomic status. Additionally, I break these results down by party spending and party identification, and find differentiated results for the disaggregated spending measures when interacted with party identification of the respondents. Generally, these results show how the electoral environment shapes interpersonal communication.

This research continues as follows: First I discuss literature surrounding political discussion and campaigns' effects on citizens. I then present our theory and hypotheses of how advocacy is triggered by campaigns. Next, I outline the data and methods. Last, I discuss the implications of our findings.

Political Discussion and Advocacy

Advocates try to influence the vote of others, by either trying to get an un-mobilized person to vote, or trying to actually get someone to change their preferences or intensity of support. There is limited empirical research on this type of discussion. Democratic theorists such as Habermas (1984) and Dewey (1927) point to open, direct statements of one's opinions to others—advocacy—as being central to interpersonal communication in the public sphere. A clear articulation of one's beliefs is beneficial in discourse theory because it educates others to the reasons to support a candidate (Cooke 2000). Huckfeldt, Johnson, and Sprague (2004) show the value of the free expression of beliefs within diverse networks by demonstrating the benefits and implications of the open expression of political disagreements. Note that this diversity can come from actual disagreement about politics or merely the intensity of support for a candidate. There can also be diversity in whether or not the person being advocated to is motivated to be involved in the campaign at all. Regardless, the purpose of advocacy is to get someone to change something, and that usually requires an articulation of one's ideas. The purpose of this project is to explicitly test the determinants of this important subset of political communication, which has heretofore been ignored or lumped in with discussion.

Most interpersonal political communication research has focused on general aspects of political discussion, such as the amount of discussion. The problem with this as a measure is that it is both a low bar for citizen engagement and eschews other more complicated but important ways to communicate politics. The political networks literature, for instance, uses congruence of network beliefs about certain issues or candidate preferences to estimate the effect of networks on vote choice or policy positions (e.g., Huckfeldt and Sprague 1995). While extremely interesting, this overlooks other styles of communication, such as advocacy. Furthermore, most research on a closely linked concept— persuasion—is predicated on elite persuasion of the masses (Koch 1998; Mutz, Brody, and Sniderman 1996; Zaller 1992), the status of the speaker, the attention and cognitive capability of the listener, and the quality or strength of argument (Cobb and Kulklinski 1997; Lau, Smith, and Fiske 1991; Petty and Cacioppo 1984). Advocacy, however, merits more investigation because advocating for a candidate requires citizens to elaborate on their beliefs about candidates or issues specifically, and is a dialogue of real-world importance.

Speaking out to those who might not share your beliefs or level of intensity can be a daunting task. Nonetheless, political theorists and social scientists assert that vibrant political discussion will lead to increased political participation, representation, and improve democracy generally (Huckfeldt, Johnson, and Sprague 2004; Mill 1859; Button and Mattson 1999; Simon 2002). Even though some research suggests that disagreeing ideologies in networks decrease participation (Mutz 2002a, 2006; Eveland and Hively 2009), advocacy does not necessarily entail ideological disagreement. As previously mentioned, one could advocate to those who have not yet committed. Advocates will try to convince others to either become active or—if active already—to increase their level of support, or even to change sides when they feel that there is a legitimate chance their preferred candidate can win.

Thus, while I examine other systemic and individual influences that encourage greater advocacy, and I particularly focus on campaigns. I argue that campaign activity provides an impetus for advocates to feel compelled into action. I assert that campaigns are a macro-level cue from which advocates get motivation.

Campaigns and Democracy

Research indicates that campaigns are generally beneficial for citizen competence and political engagement (Coleman and Manna 2000; Freedman, Franz, and Goldstein 2004). For example, Rosenstone and Hansen (1993) demonstrate that as voter mobilization activities decrease, so does voter participation. Furthermore, campaigns are also periods of significant learning for citizens (Benoit, Hansen, and Verser 2003; Patterson 2002). Specific to campaign finance, Coleman and Manna (2000) show that campaign spending in congressional races has myriad benefits for citizens. Spending increases policy-specific knowledge, awareness of issues surrounding the election, and boosts competitiveness by making voters question assumptions about incumbents (Coleman and Manna 2000). Coleman (2001) also notes that these benefits are not concentrated among more politically engaged groups. The benefits of spending—higher candidate knowledge, or issue awareness—are distributed evenly across socioeconomic groups and political ideologies (Coleman 2001). This is important because the struggle citizens typically have with political knowledge is well documented (Bartels 1996; Kulklinski, et al. 2000; Delli, Carpini, and Keeter 1996). Furthermore, we know that citizens look for vigorous campaign spending to discern the competitiveness of an election (Huckfeldt, Carmines, Mondak, and Zeemering 2007; Wolak 2009).

Campaign spending is now in the billions of dollars (Borst 2006; see also The Center for Responsive Politics 2010), so it is crucial to understand fully how this spending influences democratic practices. Candidates spend to increase their vote share (Nagler and Leighley 1992), inform voters (Freedman, Franz, and Goldstein 2004), and—in the case of incumbents—keep control of the office they hold (Green 2006). Even though spending per se does not equal higher rates of turnout in the aggregate (Geer and Lau 2006), campaign resources influence outcomes—the more money candidates have, the better they do (see, e.g., Partin 2002). These results are found in models that account for endogenous relationships, as better candidates may receive more donations (Erikson and Palfrey 1998; Gerber 1998; Rekkas 2007). One common worry is that campaign spending is often used for negative advertisements, which is a hotly debated aspect of money in American politics. Some scholars find that negative campaigns decrease turnout and make citizens more cynical about politics (Ansolabehere, et al. 1994; Ansolabehere and Iyengar 1996). Others in this debate claim that negative advertisements, indeed ad spending generally, actually mobilizes the electorate (Geer and Lau 2005; Geer 2006; Goldstein and Freedman 2002), so perhaps even negative advertising may incite more advocacy. What is notable about the literature on campaign effects is the dearth of research on how campaigns interact with interpersonal communication.

Scholarship on campaign spending has generally centered on the marginal effects of each additional dollar spent on behalf of candidates (Green 2006). I add to this literature, and advance it in a new way. I examine if campaign spending has a positive externality that turns citizens into localized advocates for political candidates. Based on these ideas, I posit that campaign intensity makes advocacy more likely. That is to say, when there is a highly active campaign, advocates should feel more motivation to speak out. These active campaigns provide stimuli that should promote citizens to become advocates. Campaign spending is a hallmark of vigorous campaigns, and may create a macro-environment that pushes citizens to advocate their positions. After all, campaigns are, at their core, "forums for public interpersonal communication" (Simon 2002, p. 11). It is possible then that campaign spending will correlate with a greater likelihood of advocacy.

Our first hypothesis, then, is that campaign spending will correlate with a greater likelihood of a citizen advocating for their preferred candidate. Also, I expect that when compared to independents partisans will be more likely to be stimulated by spending from their party, as the campaigns often target base voters. Although, an alternative hypothesis would be that the spending by the opposing party motivates partisans to advocate for their candidate, because they feel like they are going to lose. Empirically, I can possibly adjudicate between these competing hypotheses with the analysis below. Our second hypothesis, then, is that if the campaign spending is broken down by party, I expect there to be partisan differentials in the predicted likelihood of advocacy based on the cues that this spending provides different partisans.

Data

I use NES survey data from United States presidential election years from 1976–2008 to model the causes of advocacy. The data, questionnaires, response rates, and detailed information on the survey methodology are available at the NES website.

The political advocacy dependent variable is measured with a question that asks the respondent, "During the campaign, did you talk to any people and try to show them why they should vote for or against one of the parties or candidates?," coded (1) if yes and (0) if no. In general, around 35 percent of the population advocates for a candidate or party in presidential election years. This shows that advocacy is a real part of political communication, but there are possible issues with this measure. One issue is that the question does not probe the frequency of advocacy. As I know that frequency of discussion leads to more participation generally (Verba, Brady, and Schlozman 1995; Huckfeldt and Sprague 1995; Mutz 2002b; Eveland and Hively 2009), it would be useful to see if the frequency of advocacy demonstrates similar results. At present, I cannot because the NES question specifically noting the frequency of advocacy is not asked in all surveys used in this dataset. Thus, I use the dichotomous measure. The second issue is that our measure cannot account for the type of advocacy—homogeneous or heterogeneous. This means that I do not know if the respondent advocates to someone who is like-minded politically (homogeneous) or someone who is opposed to the respondent's position (heterogeneous). As a result, there are interesting questions I cannot answer at this time about this topic. Nonetheless, this general measure of advocacy has yet to be tested in political science, so the need for basic research on this subject is clear.

The independent variables combine objective campaign spending data with survey data. The campaign spending data are from La Raja (2008: 31). These are normalized to 2004 dollars and listed in hundreds of millions of dollars. These data only include measures of hard money for each party's presidential candidate. These are the total expenditures reported to the FEC from the candidate's campaign. The 2008 data was added to the La Raja (2008) data, which only went to 2004. Interestingly, these data show a Republican advantage in hard money in every election, except 2008. In 2008, Democrats broke the Republican hard money advantage by utilizing the Internet as a fundraising tool, and also benefited from a highly unpopular incumbent Republican president. From these data, I also break the total hard spending (THS) variable into its Republican Hard Spending (RHS) for Republican presidential candidates and Democratic Hard Spending (DHS) values for Democratic presidential candidates.

I also include control variables that may influence advocacy. A more competitive race may make citizens advocate more because the electoral outcome is not clear and they may feel they could sway the outcome. Our variable, Competitiveness, measures the closeness of the presidential election by calculating the final difference in electoral percentage between the Republican and Democratic candidates as a proxy for overall competitiveness in actual votes (not Electoral College votes) for each state in each election. This is an accepted proxy for competitiveness, as it represents a concrete evaluation of the closeness of the electoral outcomes and it is commonly used (see, e.g., Mayhew 1974). Because this is measured at the state level, I will use a hierarchical logistic model (HLM) below to account for the clustering of respondents within states.

I also include a dichotomous measure of whether there is an incumbent president in the presidential election, as incumbents may have stronger mobilization teams and campaign infrastructure with deeper attachments from voters, all of which should lead to greater advocacy in years with an incumbent running. Political interest and involvement of the respondent may also influence advocacy. Interest in politics may make someone more likely to advocate, and here that is measured by whether the respondent is not much (0), somewhat (1), or very interested (2) in politics. Partisan attachment should make the respondent more likely to advocate. Strength of Partisanship is coded as not attached to any party (0), slightly (1), somewhat (2), and strongly partisan (3). Having efficacy and trusting others may facilitate advocacy because these individuals are likely to feel that their input on behalf of a candidate can make a difference. Efficacy is measured with the NES standard index of the respondent's feelings toward their ability to influence politics and how well they feel government responds to citizens' concerns (Cronbach's alpha = 0.6353). I measure generalized trust with a question asking "Generally speaking, would you say that most people can be trusted (coded 1) or that you can't be too careful in dealing with people (coded 0)." In addition, television usage may stimulate engagement in the campaign and thereby promote advocacy, because television is the prime medium for campaigns to activate and inform their followers (Brians and Wattenberg 1996; Freedman, Franz, and Goldstein 2004; Mondak 1995). To measure television usage, I include the NES variable that asks respondents the number of nights per week they watch television nightly news (0–7). Political knowledge is measured with a standard open-ended ranking of political knowledge, coded ordinally from 0-5. Retrospective evaluations are important for vote choice during elections (Fiorina 1981), so it might also affect advocacy because voters who perceive their economic situation to be good probably want to keep it that way. Thus, I control for retrospective evaluations with the NES retrospective variable asking if the past year has been poor (0), the same (1), or better (2) for the respondent's family economically. Ideology also may have an impact on the likelihood of advocacy, and it is measured on a seven-point scale, conservative being the highest. I also control for being male, black, Latino, income (in $5,000 increments), having foreign-born parents, education by degree attainment, and age. Just as these variables have been effective at predicting other types of political activity (Verba, Schlozman, and Brady 1995; Huckfeldt and Sprague 1995), I believe that they may affect advocacy.

The fundamental claim is that advocacy is a subset of discussion, and that advocacy is correlated with processes that may not actually affect the amount of discussion. I make no a priori clams, however, as to whether discussion is a cause of advocacy or not. Thus, I create models that include and exclude discussion. To do this, I have two measures at our disposal. The first is the NES variable used in 6 of the 8 elections in our dataset. This question is a simple dichotomous variable asking if the respondent discussed politics with friends or family during the election (coded 1 if yes, 0 if no). Another, more interesting variable asks respondents the frequency with which they discussed politics with friends or family (0–7, reflecting days of the week respondents discussed politics and the campaign). Unfortunately, this variable is asked in only two of the elections I study, so I are unable to use it in the full analysis.

Methods

To estimate our results, I create multilevel logistic regression models of the dichotomous measure of advocacy. Logistic regression models may be problematic with these data, which are clustered in states, and over different election years. The survey data are clustered by states and election years, and I need to account for this clustering which violates the IID assumptions of regression modeling (Wooldridge 2002, p. 6). Our data incorporate state-level and year-level variables as well as individual-level variables that vary for each individual. Theoretically I know there is a significant potential for clustering because Electoral College calculations are done on the state level and in different election-year environments. This is also statistically justified, as a likelihood-ratio test showed significant clustering in the data.

HLM, sometimes called multilevel models, are becoming common (see Gelman and Hill [2007] for a detailed description). The basic idea of multilevel modeling is to reduce bias when data are organized in a nested hierarchy of successively higher-level units (Raudenbush and Bryk 2002). When data are in this nested structure, it violates the independence assumption in linear models, and can induce a type of bias. Here, I control for the between-state and between-year variances as well as the between-individual variance (Wooldridge 2002, p. 6). Note that these are not panel data because the dependent variable is only recorded once for different survey respondents in every election, and not over time. The data are, however, clustered in states and in election years, which may cause circumstances that influence the level of advocacy. Note, also, that I find similar results from logistic regression models with and without clustered robust standard errors, and a bivariate probit model that simultaneously predicts discussion and advocacy. Importantly, endogeneity—a perennial concern for social science generally—is not a significant concern for us here. It is highly unlikely that people advocating to their neighbors or friends about a political candidate or campaign would encourage a campaign to spend more money than they plan to spend in the first place. However, it might be the case that an underlying cause of both campaign spending and advocacy is present, such as a competitive campaign. That is controlled for here, so any concerns about significant endogeneity or bi-causal relationships should be mitigated.

Results

Now I examine the HLM with predictors at three levels for political advocacy. The first model is a baseline model which omits political discussion, while the second includes it as a predictor of advocacy. Also, as the degrees of freedom are low at level three, I show models 1 and 2 without the incumbent variable and model 3 with it. Level one has individual-level predictors of advocacy, level two has a state-level predictor, and level three has election-year predictors. All three models show that the level-three predictors explain around 30 percent of the variance in the likelihood of advocating, which can be seen by the intraclass correlation (ICC) statistic. All specifications show that political advocacy correlates with increased campaign spending, although with the incumbent variable added in model 3 the p-value for spending is .06. As there are only six elections covered in this model (because the discussion variable is asked in only six of these eight elections) the inclusion of another predictor at level three slightly raises the p-value from .04 in the first two models to .06 in model 3. Thus, I can be reasonably confident that stimulation in the macro-level environment correlates with greater interpersonal communication about politics. This supports our hypothesis that advocacy is an outcome of campaign spending. Moreover, the correlation of spending with advocacy remains even when controlling for state-level differences in electoral competitiveness. At level three, I find that incumbency does not have an impact. At level two, we see that competitiveness is signed in the wrong direction for our theory, but has a p-value around .20 in these models. I suspect that more data would reveal a clearer correlation with competitiveness, but at this time I cannot offer supportive evidence for this relationship with these data.

Among the level one variables, our predictions are generally borne out. I see that political discussion has a substantial and positive correlation with advocacy. Less substantial, but reliable and positive effects on advocacy are observed for television usage and political knowledge. Also consistent with our expectations, greater interest, partisanship, efficacy and being male also correlate with greater advocacy in all models. These results match our expected predictions. Greater age, political trust, being foreign born and being black have a negative correlation with advocacy in all models. The remaining control variables were signed in the anticipated direction but fell short of conventional levels of statistical significance.

Also of interest is the relative effect of different levels of campaign spending. Interpreting the coefficients, I see that if the average election changed from one standard deviation below the mean of campaign spending to one standard deviation above the mean, ceteris paribus, that would correlate with around a six-percentage-point increase in advocacy rates, and is significant at the $p < .05$ level. This suggests that campaign spending is one way in which macro-level input can relate with political interpersonal communication.

To this point I have only tested the theory that aggregate spending by presidential candidates creates the macro-environment that encourages advocacy. However, what is the effect of Republican and Democratic candidate spending specifically, and what is the effect of Republican and Democratic spending on each type of partisan? I test hypothesis 2 in table 7.2 with two models. Model 1 is the general model to test the effect of spending by each party generally. Model 2 tests the effect spending by party with interaction terms for respondent's party identification. Both models show that the level-three predictors here explain around 17 percent of the variance in the likelihood of advocating, which can be seen by the ICC statistic. Included in these models is a partisanship variable which controls for the strength of partisanship, so "0" is an independent and "3" is a strong partisan. Models estimated without partisanship as a control have essentially identical results. In the interest of full specification I have partisan strength presented here. These models in table 7.2 test if Republican or Democratic respondents vary in advocacy by the level of spending by Republican and Democratic candidate spending.

Table 7.1: Multi-Level Model: Determinants of Political Advocacy

Variable	1	(SE)	2	(SE)	3	(SE)
Level 3						
THS	0.001*	(0.000)	0.001*	(0.000)	0.0009+	(0.0005)
Incumbent	--	--	--	--	0.190	(0.166)
Level 2						
Competitiveness	-0.658	(0.426)	-0.553	(0.435)	-0.550	(0.435)
Level 1						
Discussion	--	--	1.275***	(0.117)	1.275***	(0.117)
Strength of Partisanship	0.191	(0.034)	0.183***	(0.034)	0.183***	(0.034)
Interest	0.717***	(0.052)	0.642***	(0.054)	0.641***	(0.054)
Efficacy	0.054*	(0.021)	0.042+	(0.022)	0.042+	(0.022)
Television	0.640***	(0.109)	0.540***	(0.111)	0.542***	(0.111)
Retrospective	-0.023	(0.040)	-0.023	(0.040)	-0.024	(0.040)
Political Knowledge	0.238***	(0.038)	0.193***	0.039	0.194***	(0.039)
Political Trust	-0.007***	(0.002)	-0.007***	(0.002)	-0.007***	(0.002)
Ideology	0.045*	(0.022)	0.047*	(0.023)	0.047*	(0.023)
Black	-0.335**	(0.112)	-0.312**	(0.113)	-0.311**	(0.113)
Latino	-0.138	0.150	-0.090	(0.152)	-0.086	(0.153)
Income	0.056+	(0.031)	0.043	(0.032)	0.042	(0.032)
Education	-0.026	(0.041)	-0.058	(0.042)	-0.058	(0.042)
Age	-0.015***	(0.002)	-0.012***	(0.002)	-0.012***	(0.002)
Male	0.134*	(0.063)	0.148*	(0.064)	0.148*	(0.064)
Parents For. Born	-0.176+	(0.091)	-0.162+	(0.092)	-0.164+	(0.092)
Intercept	-3.711***	(0.266)	-4.432***	(0.290)	-4.622***	(0.331)
N	7574		5092		5092	
$\chi 2$	259.92**		252.44**		252.98**	
ICC	0.267		0.328		0.271	

Note: Cells represent unstandardized coefficients and standard errors estimated with HLM Logit Link Function for determinants of political advocacy in presidential elections from 1976–2008.

In Model 1 DHS is positive and significant, indicating that when Democratic spending goes up so too does the likelihood of individuals advocating. Republican spending is insignificant. This finding suggests hypothesis 2 was correct, and that spending creates cues of a competitive electoral environment and advocacy is activated. Because Republicans held the hard money advantage in every election except 2008, increases in Democratic spending may indicate increases in the competitive nature of the election to average citizens, even though the actual level of competitiveness was found to be not significant.

Table 7.2: Multi-Level Model: Determinants of Political Advocacy with Interactions

Variable	1	(SE)	2	(SE)
Level 3				
RHS	-0.002	(0.001)	0.000	(0.002)
DHS	0.003+	(0.001)	-0.000	(0.002)
Incumbent	0.114	(0.165)	0.112	(0.164)
Level 2				
Competitiveness	-0.049	(0.321)	-0.050	(0.321)
Level 1				
RHS x Republican	--	--	-0.004+	(0.002)
RHS x Democrat	--	--	-0.005*	(0.002)
DHS x Republican	--	--	0.003	(0.002)
DHS x Democrat	--	--	0.004+	(0.002)
Republican	0.120	(0.119)	0.082	(0.122)
Democrat	0.029	(0.119)	-0.011	(0.122)
Strength of Partisanship	0.201***	(0.034)	0.204***	(0.034)
Interest	0.678***	(0.042)	0.681***	(0.042)
Efficacy	0.002***	(0.000)	0.002***	(0.000)
Political Trust	-0.006***	(0.001)	-0.006***	(0.001)
Television	0.604***	(0.092)	0.606***	(0.092)
Retrospective	-0.015	(0.032)	-0.016	(0.032)
Political Knowledge	0.271***	(0.031)	0.271***	(0.032)
Ideology	0.012	(0.020)	0.008	(0.020)
Black	-0.311**	(0.097)	-0.310**	(0.098)
Latino	-0.123	(0.144)	-0.120	(0.144)
Income	0.035	(0.025)	0.034	(0.025)
Education	0.019	(0.033)	0.019	(0.033)
Age	-0.015***	(0.001)	-0.015***	(0.001)
Male	0.166**	(0.051)	0.169**	(0.051)
Parents Foreign Born	-0.098	(0.073)	-0.098	(0.073)
Intercept	-3.548***	(0.205)	-4.432***	(0.290)
N	7574		7574	
$\chi 2$	361.42***		362.16***	

Note: Cells in Table 7.2 represent unstandardized coefficients and standard errors estimated with HLM Logit Link Function for determinants of political advocacy in Presidential elections from 1976 to 2008.

Model 2 in table 7.2 displays the interactions of spending by campaigns and the respondents' partisan attachments. Given the nature of the data, these are cross-level interactions, where respondent partisanship (Republican or Democrat) is a level-1 variable, and spending is a level-3 variable. The interaction terms for Democratic partisans are both significant, and in the expected directions. RHS x Democrat is negative and significant, while DHS x Democrat is positive and significant. These findings suggest that Democrats are activated to advocate when their party's presidential candidate spends increasing amounts of money, but are deactivated when Republicans spend increasing amounts of money. However, the RHS x Republican interaction term is also negative and significant as well, while the DHS x Republican interaction term is not significant, which presents somewhat mixed results for Republicans and spending. These results suggest that impact of campaign spending on advocacy is going to be mediated by the differential level of spending by each party, and how that differential interacts with partisans. The mixed results for Republicans and clearer results for Democratic partisans suggest more work is needed on why spending correlates differentially with partisans. Additionally, the competitiveness measure is once again signed in the wrong direction, but is still insignificant. Thus, there is little I can say about variable at this time, but more data would likely provide better leverage for our theory.

Conclusion

I examined the correlates of political advocacy, which is necessary for political discussion to create rationalized discourse. The clear articulation of a position—what I term advocacy here—is foundational to nearly all theories of deliberative democracy. Chiefly, this project demonstrated that as campaign spending increases, so too does the likelihood of an individual becoming an advocate for their candidate. Advocacy correlates with campaign spending even while controlling for other likely determinants, such as SES and attitudinal variables. I theorized that active campaigns stimulate citizens to speak out for the candidate they support, and I find that greater campaign spending has a positive and significant correlation with advocacy. This project is important for two reasons. First, it is important to demonstrate that there is an under-studied area of interpersonal communication that has serious implications for practical politics. To date, almost all research on interpersonal communication has focused on determinants of political discussion generally (Huckfeldt and Sprague 1995; Mutz 2006). However, in doing so, scholars have either overlooked advocacy or conflated it with discussion. The second part of this project concerns the differential impact of campaign spending by party and party identification. I show that greater Democratic campaign spending correlates with greater advocacy generally. I also find disproportionate effects based on party identification, whereby those who are Democrats are activated to advocate when their party's Presidential candidate spends increasing amounts of money, but are deactivated when Republicans spend increasing amounts of money.

Chapter 8
The Electoral System and Political Discussion

Continuing the analysis of how the electoral environment affects political discussion, I look at how the electoral system—how votes are counted—influences political discussion. To get at this subject is difficult, because the electoral system changes rarely. To do so, I now focus on a case study of Oregon and its change to an all-absentee systems, where all voters vote by mail. The vote-by-mail reform provides a simple and inexpensive way to encourage voter turnout. But does it transform other types of political participation? Poor and marginalized groups benefit most from the change, perhaps because they have more difficulties getting to a polling place. Do these same groups also have higher levels of social capital after the reform? The pamphlet "Oregon Secretary of State Vote-by-Mail Frequently Asked Questions" lists another goal of the reform as "allowing more time for people to study issues and candidates before marking the ballot" (Elections Office 2000). My theory is that the reform makes possible a style of voting that engenders political discussion because of its open style, which is no longer a secret ballot. The secret ballot dampens political participation and with it community involvement and civic engagement (Barbalet 2002). Recent scholarship finds that civic engagement and community involvement are very important for society. The social capital literature finds that more engagement and involvement can greatly improve a community (Putnam 2001). Social capital is defined as the amount of civic engagement and community involvement in society (Coleman 1990, Putnam 1993, 2001). This chapter will determine if voting by mail has changed the way people feel and act toward their society, by testing its impact on political discussion.

Do voters who vote by mail do so in more isolation than those at a polling place? Thompson (2004) posits that voting by mail limits electoral civic
engagement by preventing the temporal norm of simultaneity on Election Day.
He argues that "voting together openly on the same day . . . is different . . . from
the private transaction" of voting by mail (Thompson 2004, p. 58). Why is voting at home more private than at a polling place? The chief benefit of the polling
place is that it offers a private space for a secret ballot. Once the curtain shuts,
the polling booth cuts the voter off from friends, family, and sources of information. Voting by mail offers the potential social benefits of discussing your
choices "together openly" with friends and family as you mark your ballot. The
open process of voting by mail may be more social than the atomized polling
booth experience. Thompson says "voting alone may be worse than bowling
alone" (Thompson 2004, p. 58). But whether voting at home equates to voting
alone is a question that needs empirical testing. The open process of voting by
mail may promote interpersonal communication, and, thus, may also be a communal experience. This study tests whether voting by mail increases political
discussion by creating a Poisson model of NES data from 1998 and 2000. I find
that voting by mail leads to more political discussion, while controlling for political interest, party ID, mobilization, media exposure, feelings of efficacy, and
socioeconomic differences. This evidence supports the theory that voting by
mail offers voters a more open and deliberatory system and does not necessarily
mean voting alone.

This research answers questions important to electoral system reform
and democratic theories of political communication. For electoral system reformers, one of the leading critiques offered by opponents of voting by mail is
that there is a loss of polling booth camaraderie when we do not vote together on
Election Day. The social function of the polling place had a powerful allure
since America has declining civic engagement (Putnam 2001). Recent scholarship finds that civic engagement and community involvement are very important
for society. Thus, politicians and the public are naturally wary of approving reforms that harm civil society, especially something as honored as the secret ballot. Yet, voting by mail has many beneficial effects such as increased turnout,
lower costs, and greater participation from the marginalized that make this a
valuable potential reform for the United States (Southwell 2004, Karp and Ban-
ducci 2001, and Bradbury 2003). If voting by mail offers civic engagement benefits through increased political discussion, then this should also be considered
in debates on electoral system reform along with any negative effects. Heretofore, the relationship between voting by mail and political discussion was ignored. Studying this relationship provides empirical evidence for electoral reformers to use when considering its impact on civic engagement (which I cite
below shows is increased by political discussion).

Also, the research addresses a key theoretical debate in the social capital literature, which is whether or not institutional design can promote civic engagement. The social capital literature finds that more engagement and involvement can greatly improve a community (Putnam 2001). Social capital is

defined as the amount of trust, civic engagement, and community involvement in society (Coleman 1988, Putnam 2001). In doing away with the secret ballot, I argue that the institutional change to voting by mail promotes political discussion, and, in turn, civic engagement and social capital. An example of the possible creation of social capital in the open ballot system is that some churches in Oregon invite members to come and discuss the issues and candidates and mark their ballots together during election week (Dreker 1998).

Before determining the impact of the electoral system on the amount of political discussions, it first needs to be shown that political discussion is beneficial for civil society. Below, this study confirms that the introduction of the secret ballot reduced America's political deliberation, suggesting that the open system of voting by mail might lead to more political discussions. Then, I review current research that shows that political discussions lead to civic engagement. Next, I test whether voting by mail promotes political discussion during the election week. Finally, I show how these arguments bear on current electoral reform debates.

The Secret Ballot and Limited Participation

Voting by mail is not necessarily a secret ballot as voters can mark their mail-in ballots together or alone. The secret ballot is one source of America's decreasing political participation from the nineteenth to the twentieth century. There are two sets of theories on the Australian ballot system and its dampening effects on political participation. One is the vote market hypothesis which "assumes secret ballots were designed to end the buying and selling of votes. The secrecy the new ballot provided discouraged candidates from buying votes they could no longer verify, disproportionately affecting poor voters who would respond to this loss of payments by voluntarily abstaining." (Heckelman 2000) Another is the strategic disfranchisement hypothesis that posits, "blacks and illiterates were specifically targeted for disfranchisement. The new ballots were expected to be more difficult for these voters to use and they would then be effectively prevented from participating in the active electorate." (Heckelman 2000) Either way, participation decreases with a secret ballot. This debate ignores the change to secret ballots also brought a loss of civic engagement and access to information about politics.

Barbalet (2002) shows that the secret ballot had more impact than reducing fraud or increasing the difficulty of voting for illiterates. Barbalet says that the secret ballot is "better explained by its effects on working class organization and crowd control" (Barbalet 2002, p. 135). The secret ballot not only separates the voter from undue influence but conversely the enlightening influence of his peers. Barbalet (p. 137) quotes Rokkan, who says that:

> In secret voting the individual adult is cut off from all his roles in the subordi-
> nate systems of the household, the neighborhood, the work organization, the
> church and the civil association and set to act excessively in the abstract role of
> a citizen of the overall political system; there will be no feedback for what he
> does in this anonymous role to what he does in the other roles

Thus, Barbalet concludes that low turnout is evidence of "alienation from
the electoral process," which became less social (Barbalet 2002, p. 138). The
secret ballot limits political communication along with other more negative influences on voters. Sanders (1997) suggests that deliberation produces emotion-
alism in politics, which is not beneficial for civic life, often leading to pressuring
and contention. A concern with voting by mail is "undue influence" from family, peers, or bosses on a voter's ability to freely choose. Studies show, however,
that voting by mail in Oregon did not lead to undue influence (Southwell and
Burchett 2000). Voting by mail makes it is easier for the emotions of a campaign to spur the voter to discussion and action, due to their access to information in a potentially deliberatory setting. I theorize that the open system of
voting by mail will encourage political discussion when compared to secret-
ballot polling-booth voters or non-voters. This increase in discussion in turn
increases civic engagement. I include non-voters to test whether electoral involvement can affect discussion in any form.

Political Discussions Create Civic Engagement

Deliberation has long been recognized as a positive influence on democracy
(Rousseau 1973, Arendt 1970, Barber 1984, Rawls 1980, 1993, Habermas 1984,
1987, Benhabib 1996, Cohen 1997, Rorty 1996, Dworkin 1986, and Cooke
2000). However, many recent studies focus on political discussion, rather than
deliberation (e.g., Conover, Searing, and Crewe 2002, or Huckfeldt, Mendez,
and Osborn 2004). These studies find that most people do not deliberate, which
is usually defined as formal public debates. Instead they have more informal
political discussion with friends, family, and neighbors (Conover, Searing, and
Crewe 2002). These studies find that political discussions have many of the
same positive benefits that democratic theorists assign to the more formal deliberation (Conover, Searing, and Crewe 2002). For example, knowledge of politics increases when people discuss politics (Price, Capella, and Nir 2002). Also,
discussants vote at higher levels (Linimon and Joslyn 2002), and have more incentive to join political movements (McAdam and Paulsen 1993). One important study by Brown and Brown (2003) shows that social capital increases
with more political discussion. And, of course, since most measures of social
capital include voter turnout as part of their index (e.g., Putnam 2001). Since
voting by mail increases turnout, it, then, also increases social capital by most
measures in addition to any discussant effects. Perhaps this is due to the trust
that develops when discussing politics openly, rather than harboring unspoken

feelings. Brown and Brown (2003) show that when black churches have members who discuss politics, they are much more likely to volunteer and participate in both electoral and non-electoral politics. Brown and Brown, and other scholars, find that many people have contentious disagreements within informal political discussions, which signifies that these are free exchanges of feelings and ideas. For example, Ikeda and Huckfeldt (2001) find that people are often aware of the differences in the partisanship of the people they discuss politics with. They show that this is important because people then have had informative discussions, instead of assuming that their family members think as they do. Also, Price, Capella, and Nir (2002) show that people often have contentious political discussions, which increase their knowledge of politics. Cooke (2000) posits that there are five effects of political discussion (educative, communicative, procedural, egalitarian, and contextual), and all make democracies work better. In sum, discussion of politics is beneficial for democracy and aids in the creation of social capital.

Data

I test the impact of the electoral system on election week political discussions using the NES data from 1998 and 2000. There is a well-known difference in participation in presidential and mid-term elections that might be reflected in the amount of political discussion. To examine this difference, and make sure these effects are found in more than one election, I test data from both the 1998 and 2000 elections. The NES asks the same questions used below for both surveys. The variable *Political Discussions* counts the number of days the respondent had political discussions in the week before the election, coded zero to seven. *Vote Method* measures how the respondent voted. It is coded zero if someone did not vote, one if they voted in a polling booth, and two if they voted by mail. Other factors could influence the amount of political discussion, and if these factors are affecting more voters using one of these methods, then these factors could bias the results. For example, paying attention to the campaign increases political discussion (Bennet, Flickinger, and Rhine 2000). To control for this, the variable *Campaign Attention* measures the respondent's self-described interest in the election, coded from one if high interest to five for low interest. Media exposure also promotes political discussions (Bennet, Flickinger, and Rhine 2000). *News Attention* measured the amount of media exposure of the respondent, coded from one if low exposure to five for high exposure. Republicans vote absentee more, and this partisan difference could lead to differences in the level of political discussion. *Party ID is* coded one for strong Democrat to seven for strong Republican. If someone feels alienated from the political system, they might not be motivated to speak about politics. The variable *Efficacy* measured how much power the respondent feels he or she has over the system, coded from one with little power to five with much power. Someone might also speak about politics if they are enlightened to the issues of the campaign by parties or others political groups during the election. *Mobilization* is a dichotomous variable that is coded as one if a party or political group contacted the respondent, and zero if not. Those knowledgeable about politics might be more likely to speak about it. Along with political knowledge, education may cause a person to become rhetorically skillful and willing to discuss politics (Bennet, Flickinger, and Rhine 2000). *Education* is measured from those without a high school degree coded as one, to those with a postgraduate degree coded as nine. Research shows that the elderly discuss politics less often, so I control for *Age,* which is measured from one to seven (Bennet, Flickinger, and Rhine 2000). The labor movement was active in these election campaigns, and belonging to a union may increase the likelihood of political discussions. *Union Membership* is a dichotomous variable with one being a member, and zero if not. *Income* positively affects discussion levels; here it is measured in increasing categories of $5,000 (Bennet, Flickinger, and Rhine 2000). *Race* affects political discussions, with whites engaging in more conversations (Bennet, Flickinger, and Rhine 2000). Here, whites are coded as one, and non-whites are zero. Men have more political discussions; here *Gender* is a dichotomous variable where male equals one, and female is coded as two.

Methods

Several studies use a similar measure of political discussion; a survey question that asks how many political discussions people had in the last week (e.g., Bennet, Flickinger, and Rhine 2000). These studies use an Ordinary Least Squares (OLS) regression model on this dependent variable. The number of political discussions, however, is event count data. Event count data are integer counts of observable events or things, examples of which are the number of presidential vetoes, the number of wars experienced by a country, and the number of times someone has moved. Thus, it is clear that an events count model is a better choice for modeling the amount of political discussions per week than an OLS regression model.

Findings

The results show that voters who vote by mail have more political discussion than those in the polling booth, or non-voters in the 1998 and 2000 elections. The *Vote Method* variable has a significant positive affect on political discussion in both elections. This means that voters who vote by mail have more conversations than those who vote at a polling booth, and even more than those who do not vote, while holding the other variables constant. Non-voters are less likely to discuss politics even after controlling for political interest, confirming that electoral involvement does affect the amount of political conversations. There is a general decrease in the number of conversations in the 1998 mid-term election, which confirms that mid-term elections have less public interest. This is, also, reflected in lower turnout in those elections. The other significant variables match the theoretical predictions. Campaign attention increases political discussions (please note that the variable *Campaign Attention* is coded with a lower score equating to higher interest). Political discussions decrease with age, and increase with education and income. In 2000, whites have slightly more political conversations, and so do Republicans.

Table 8.1 presents the results of the Clarify simulation that shows that when holding all other variables at their mean, those who vote by mail in 2000 have about half of a political discussion more than those who voted in a polling booth. Non-voters have about one less political conversation than those who vote by mail. Interestingly, there is a smaller differential in the 1998 election with those who vote by mail having about a third of a political discussion more than those who voted in a polling booth. Non-voters had about one half of a political conversation less than those who vote by mail in 1998.

Table 8.1: Differences in Level of Discussion

Quantity of Interest	Mean	Std. Err.	[95% Conf. Interval]	
2000				
Vote By Mail	4.79	.226	4.34	5.24
Polling Booth	4.34	.082	4.19	4.52
1998				
Vote By Mail	2.46	.158	2.15	2.78
Polling Booth	2.16	.062	2.04	2.28

Table 8.1: Cells represent the results of a simulation created by Clarify. These simulations hold all other control variables (political interest, party ID, mobilization, media exposure, feelings of efficacy, and socioeconomic differences) at their mean and display only a change in one unit of the causal variable.

Conclusion

As predicted, voting by mail increases turnout, and facilitates access to the polls for those who cannot make it, but has little or no partisan effects (Southwell 2004). Thompson (2004) said that these concerns should outweigh concerns for civic engagement. But to convince the public to enact needed beneficial electoral reforms, concerns over civic engagement have to be answered. If it hurts civil society, the public might not want to tamper with the secret ballot electoral system that many view as positive. In Colorado, in 2002, a similar vote only by mail referendum was rejected. This was, in part, because of a well-funded campaign to highlight the loss of civic engagement with a change to voting by mail, along with promoting fears about fraud. This research finds that these concerns are not accounting for the civil society benefits of voting by mail in promoting political discussion, which the research listed above shows leads to increased political involvement, political knowledge, and social capital.

Political theory should provide insights into problems for empirical researchers to pursue. Thompson's article provides a wealth of insight into the temporal nature of elections, and what these temporal requirements mean to electoral system reform. His conclusion, however, that voting by mail hurts civil society because it violates the norm of simultaneity, ignores the rich "togetherness" that can be achieved by voting in an open system at home. This research shows that the method of voting does affect the amount of election week political discussion, and the positive benefits of the increased deliberative environment of vote by mail.

Voting by mail is a reform that may work elsewhere. The postal system is universally available, trusted, and works well in any state. When weighing the benefits over the negative aspects, Oregon's election officials believe the reform is a success (Bradbury 2001, 2003). The United States has declining voting rates, and a simple and inexpensive reform such as voting by mail could facilitate more turnout. Importantly, in addition to an increase in general turnout, voting by mail increases turnout rates for marginalized populations (Southwell 2004). But for people to trust the new system they must believe that it will not bring negative effects to civil society. This research shows that the effect for civic engagement is not exclusively negative. Thus, the debate over voting by mail should consider its full impact on civic life.

Recent research finds that political discussions increase social capital (e.g., Brown and Brown 2004). By producing an increase in political discussions, voting by mail, thus, encourages social capital. Theories on the need for political discussion for a successful democracy are linked to a long philosophical tradition that stretches from Habermas in the twentieth century back to Rousseau, and even Aristotle (Habermas 1984, p. 10, see also Flyvbjerg p. 2). These theorists stressed that being a political animal means that we need to use political discussion to resolve our differences (Yack 1993). For example, Habermas argues for reforms of constitutions to create structures that permit and encourage political discussion (Habermas 1984, 1987). The institution-exogenous view espoused by Putnam ignores the role of government in encouraging civil society. Putnam, in fact, criticized reliance on constitutions to create the institutional structures to promote deliberation (Putnam 1993, discussed in Flyvbjerg, p. 3). Putnam suggests that institutions rarely produce a change in civic culture (Putnam 1993, p. 18). Putnam says "[t]wo centuries of constitution-writing around the world warn us . . . that designers of new institutions are often writing on water . . . That institutional reforms alter behavior is an hypothesis, not an axiom." (Putnam 1993, p. 18) The research on voting by mail supports this hypothesis, and more reforms that promote political discussion should be considered and implemented.

Can an electoral system reform change the way people participate and feel about their society? This study concludes that, yes, the reform produces a small but statistically significant increase in feelings of civic engagement and community involvement. Moreover, there are certain groups, such as the young or the disabled, which particularly benefit from this reform. Since this reform has the ability to change people's involvement in politics, then other reforms could also succeed in achieving this same goal. If public policy is shaped to be more engaging and make people feel more a part of their community, then we could expect more social capital. Although there is only a small increase of political discussion, it is important to the analysis of this reform to include these unintended effects. If other states change to voting by mail they can expect an increase in social capital and voter turnout. Moreover, considering the aforementioned cyclical potential of social capital, the reform might engender increasing levels of social capital. If people are more willing to participate after participating, then reforms that facilitate this process for only a few can have a larger impact in the long run. In the long run these unintended effects could have great consequence, as the few people motivated by voting by mail to be involved with their community will in turn motivate others. It could also be that these effects are spurious and that more time is needed to make a final conclusion. But, for now it can be tentatively concluded that the data does provide evidence that a small percentage of the population saw their civic engagement and community involvement increase due to the reform.

Chapter 9
Conclusion

This book established that political discussion increases rational decision making. Citizens often behave in ways that appear irrational (Achen and Bartels 2004, Bartels 1996, 2005). Many pundits, theorists, and scholars posit that if citizens discuss politics more, we will have a better democracy (see Bohman [1998] for a review). A large literature has established that people learn from social networks (Berelson, Lazarsfeld, and McPhee 1954, Brown and Brown 2003, Linimon and Joslyn 2002, Katz and Lazarfeld 1955, McAdam and Paulsen 1993, Price, Capella, and Nir 2002), and the logic follows that we could improve democracy if people only had more, and better, political discussion. The unstated assumption being that better understanding equates to rational choices, which this book sought to empirically verify. Under strict conditions, formal interpersonal communication has been shown to educate (Barabas 2004), but informal political discussion is more common, and is an efficient division of labor (Conover, Johnston, Searing, and Crewe 2002). Research has shown that in everyday conversation, opinion leaders teach their associates about politics (Huckfeldt 2001), and that informal political discussion is not rare (e.g., see Huckfeldt, Pappi, and Ikeda 2005). This literature finds that political discussion with knowledgable people increases knowledge of politics. Thus it seems plausible that if people receive advice on candidates from knowledgeable discussants it will help them chose the candidate that better reflects their vision of how government should act.

I found that discussion greatly benefits rational decision-making. This is shown through lab experiments and nationally representative survey data. I also show that the influence of political discussion is more beneficial than previously thought due in part to the network structure being too simplified in past theories. The autoregressive impact shows that voters make rational calculations based on multiple inputs weighted by expertise. Due to the social learning of the cognitive ability to analyze politics, political discussion creates correct voting and influences policy positions, and political attitudes such as patriotism.

This research has focused more broadly on testing how different aspects of discussion networks facilitate or hinder democratic citizenship. Understanding this may allow for public policy choices that encourage the development of institutions that are more conducive to an open and deliberative public sphere.

Institutional Influence on Discussion

If discussion is beneficial, we must also know what creates discussion. I show that change in electoral systems encourages social networking, which is type of social capital. By changing the voting system to an open style, it also increases political discussion, albeit modestly. Some would argue that social capital is outside the realm of influence of government, and argue that social capital is what influences government. Others say that institutions are needed to facilitate the development of social capital, and thus a reform like voting by mail might stimulate its creation. Changing the institutional process can produce a more engaged citizenry, which is beneficial to political life. Theories on the need for more civic engagement are linked to a long democratic philosophical tradition that stretches from Habermas in the twentieth century back to Rousseau, and even Aristotle (Bent 2000, p. 2). To be a political animal means that we have the ability to use politics to resolve our differences (Yack 1993). Civic engagement fulfills our goal of human social interaction (Valelly 1993). This theoretical line sees civic engagement as a way to mitigate rational self-interest, and thus, avoid the tragedy of the commons (Yack 1993). The ability of humans to resolve our problems by methods other than conflict is what is essential to being human, mainly because it is what separates us from animals.

Rousseau was specific on the need to create institutions that engender civic engagement (Rousseau 1960, p. 185). Civic engagement creates self-reflection about one's community. People in civil society are more likely to be thoughtful of the needs of others (Habermas 1984; 1987). It was this point from Rousseau that was so important to Hegel, Feuerbach, and subsequently to Marx. For Marx becoming a "species-being" is how humanity gains its ultimate freedom, by seeing oneself as a member of a species, and caring for its betterment (see Colletti 1975, pp. 270–400). Marx theorized that this could only happen in an institutional context that makes humans engaged in society, rather than a tool of it.

These theorists thought that seeing yourself reflected in your society—rather than a means to society's end goals—is crucial to achieving your humanity. But the process needs an institution to promote these experiences (Valelly 1993). Voting by mail may work to increase social networking and facilitates more feelings of civic engagement and community involvement. I show above that encouraging opportunities where humans can become engaged does encourage face-to-face political interaction through political discussion. As previously stated, more feelings of civic engagement and community involvement should motivate people to join groups and participate in other activities that will only further their feelings of involvement. Eventually this should lead to groups that pressure government to become more responsive. Thus, reforms can stimulate the enactment of other reforms. It is worth remembering the referendum and initiative was a reform in 1902, and it enabled the passage of the voting by mail reform. Political process reforms can enable future reforms. If voting by mail encourages more political participation, it could create an environment where more reforms are enacted in the future.

Putnam criticizes Habermas's reliance on constitutions to promote the institutional structures that enable the "life-world" (Putnam 1993, p. 18). In this life-world, scientific rationality and the efficiency of capitalism are tempered by more human concerns. Habermas desires reforms that create structures that permit and encourage participation (Habermas 1984). But Putnam counters that institutional contexts rarely produce engagement (Putnam 1993, p. 18). Putnam says "[t]wo centuries of constitution-writing around the world warn us . . . that designers of new institutions are often writing on water . . . . That institutional reforms alter behavior is an hypothesis, not an axiom." (Putnam 1993, p. 18) The research on voting by mail supports this hypothesis, and more reforms designed to promote civic engagement should be considered and implemented.

Although many recent studies show the benefits of civic engagement for communities and participating individuals, the social mechanisms that cause collective action have not received the attention they deserve (Ostrom 1998). Before we can promote civil society, we first must know what causes people to participate. Social capital scholars study activities that facilitate or hinder one's opportunities to join. For example, Putnam (2000, p. 235) shows that television viewing limits the joining of voluntary associations or even family picnics. He posits that America's recent civic disengagement is caused by the dominance of television, which lowered civic association membership. Involvement in choral societies, soccer clubs, and bowling leagues are not end goals. Instead, social capital theorists desire the communal benefits created by membership in these associations. Putnam (2000) shows that aggregate participation is higher in regions with dense social networks. He suggests that interaction in face-to-face activities sponsors other community involvement.

Critics complain that there is no relevance to democracy from studying involvement in trifling informal recreational activities (Edwards 2004). Edwards (2004) doubts that informal socializing influences participation in formal community activities. However, the face-to-face interaction that Edwards finds beneficial in formal associations also occurs in informal human relations. Using Edwards's logic, backyard barbecues should increase civic engagement as well.

Gannett shows that Putnam's chief influence, Tocqueville, differentiated between formal civil and political associations—which are crucial for democracy—and social recreation. Tocqueville thought that recreation may "allow resi-
dents to "taste the enjoyments of private life" (Gannett 2003, p. 2), but is not
important for politics. Gannett states "we simply cannot equate family picnics
with various types of political engagement if we are to make our democracy
work" (Gannett 2003, p. 2). These critics, however, do not test empirically a key
concept of social network theory, that social recreation increases participation in
formal civil society. If you want to increase community involvement, and social
recreation increases involvement, then informal networks are "political" and
must be studied.

The social capital debate about whether institutions are needed to facilitate these experiences of mutual self-recognition is thus based on a fine distinction between types of institutions. Putnam cannot be anti-institutionalist because
volunteer groups are also institutions. Social capital then requires some type of
device—or conduit—to enable us to be engaged. The marketplace or civil society need not be the only spaces of societal engagement. Government can also be
a source of these spaces (Valelly 1993). The rationalized efficiency of market
economics makes it unlikely that anything other than government will provide
the institutional structures needed to promote civic engagement. The government could be coercive in processes of engagement, and this needs to be resist-
ed. But a reform like voting by mail has increased political discussion, and at the
same time did not enforce it.

Theorists frequently debate the importance of institutions to civil society (e.g., Edwards and Foley 2001 and Edwards 2004), and the research presented
in this book provides an interesting test of this debate. Jackman and Miller
(1998) describe an internal inconsistency within scholarship as to whether civic
engagement is endogenous or exogenous of institutions. They prefer James
Coleman's (1990) endogenous research approach. Putnam's work has grown
from an early (1993, p. 18) thesis that posited an exogenous-only "bottom-up"
relationship from civic culture to institutions, to a later stance (2000, p. 413) in
which institutions can promote civil society. This research tests this debate because if voting by mail and campaign activity promote discussion and advocacy,
then civic engagement is created by governmental activity, and is a determinant
of civil society.

I find that discussion was increased by these exogenous political forces,
showing that civic engagement can be developed exogenously of institutions.
Jackman and Miller's (1998) endogenous-only approach misses the important
interconnectedness of communal life. Of course, participation in institutions
may also increase one's civic engagement. Thus, influences of participation in
civil society are possibly both endogenous and exogenous of institutions. The
research proceeds as follows. After reviewing the hypotheses and data, I determine the influence of everyday casual interaction—defined as "informal social
networks."—on civic organizational involvement—defined as "formal social
networks." I find that recreational activity encourages people to join crime

watches in Japan. This research shows that informal social networking leads to participation in other areas. We cannot ignore the benefits to civil society from institution-exogenous informal social recreation. Critics of the inclusion of recreational activities in civil society measures should not dismiss their influence on traditional political participation. The research approach advocated by Gannett (2003), Edwards (2004), Edwards and Foley (2004), and Miller and Jackman (1998) ignores the impact of social interaction on institutional involvement. Both formal and informal interaction must be measured and considered to determine the full scope of civil society. These critics encourage a focus only on the institution-endogenous determinants of civil society. Ignoring real-world complications in a quest for clarity only further confuses our understanding of the multifaceted relationships we are studying. Additionally, this research suggests that although motivating involvement may be crucial to creating rational choice, increasing the density of social connectedness is where reformers should focus their energies.

Some caution, however, is needed in interpreting these results. The ability to examine this test is limited to the validity of the survey data, question wording, and methodology (Zaller 1992). This is particularly true when only examining one survey as I did here (the NES). In addition, there are limited questions of social networks in the NES data (2000, 2006, and 2008), so possible determinants cannot be included in the model. Despite these limitations, the research provides some evidence of the positive impact of institutional influence on social networking and civic life.

Network Influence Outside the United States

How about outside the United States? Much more work is needed, on comparative studies of social network influence, but some exists, and I have done some on Japan. Because of theories of East Asian network homophily, scholars often dismiss the potential of social network discussions for exposing members to diverse opinions in East Asian societies. Ken'ichi Ikeda and I demonstrated that exposure to politically heterogeneous networks is common in Japan, and that this exposure increases tolerance (Ikeda and Richey 2009).

This is not to say that discussion will always improve choices. Knowledgeable opinion leaders, however, are only one type of influential discussion partner in a discussion network. Although untested in the current literature, when political discussion amounts to pressure from social superiors to vote or think a certain way, discussion may not increase political comprehension. In an article from 2009, I tested this effect in Japan, a highly hierarchical society. I found that in Japan, discussion with social superiors increases vote similarity but does not increase knowledge.

Another article with Prof. Ikeda tested whether political discussion influences Japanese policy preference, an area that has been mostly ignored (Ikeda and Richey 2006). We showed that the likelihood of supporting a policy increases when one's social network supports a party that advocates that policy, which I replicate here with data from the United States. We also showed in a 2005 article in *Political Behavior* the influence of social networks on political participation using new Japanese survey data. The results indicated a strong positive relationship between social networking—including network hierarchy and openness—and political participation.

Finally, Ikeda and Richey (2011) examined the impact of discussion in Japan. Our book tried to answer one basic question: Is discursive participatory democracy possible in East Asia? Many who critique democracy as practiced in East Asia suggest that the Confucian political culture of these nations prevents democracy from being of the robust participatory type. At the center of this so-called "Asian-values" debate is whether there is an active political culture in East Asia that allows citizens to freely discuss, debate, and disagree about politics. We investigated this problem empirically and found that disagreement is common in Asian political discourse, and that its effects are profound, despite the cultural impetus for group harmony. The amount of political discussion in East Asia is comparable to the West; the beneficial impact also applies to Japan. This research has suggested that more cross-cultural comparative work on political discussion would be beneficial.

Areas for Future Research

Future research should continue the study of the relationship between public policy, political discussion, and voting behavior. This research also begs the question of what role institutions play in promoting civic engagement more broadly, and what is necessary for participation in one's community. Other voting reforms have been tried in other states, with some success. Comparisons between the alternative systems like voting by mail, early voting, and same-day registration would yield useful knowledge. Other research should address the politics of these reforms. Possible research questions are whether the referendum process was used to enact these reforms, and whether politicians in these states fought or supported these reforms. In a comparative perspective, it would be interesting to determine if elsewhere in the world there are reforms similar to voting by mail, and to study their effect on discussion.

The evaluation of governmental policies should be changed to consider how any policy would encourage social networking (Valelly 1993). All government policies are calculated with a cost-benefit analysis, including an estimation of environmental impact. The impact of a policy on civic engagement should be considered in a similar manner (Valelly 1993). For democracy to function properly all citizens should be fully active participants. If policies can be designed to encourage engagement they would be greatly beneficial. Although participation is not the only aspect that should influence a policy's acceptance, its effect on participation should be included as part of the calculation of costs and benefits.

Bibliography

Achen, Chris H., and Larry M. Bartels. "Musical Chairs: Pocketbook Voting and the Limits of Democratic Accountability." Paper presented at the Annual Meeting of the American Political Science Association, Chicago, 2004.

Ackerman, Bruce, and James S. Fishkin. *Deliberation Day.* New Haven: Yale University Press, 2004.

Almond, Gabriel, and Sidney Verba. *The Civic Culture.* Newbury Park, Calif: Sage Publications, 1989.

Althaus, Scott. "Information Effects in Collective Preferences." *American Political Science Review* 92, no. 3 (1998): 545-558.

Alvarez, R. Michael. *Information and Elections: Revised to Include the 1996 Presidential Election.* Ann Arbor, MI: University of Michigan Press, 1998.

Arendt, Hannah. *On Violence.* London: Allen Lane, Penguin Press, 1970.

Barbalet, Jack M. "Secret Voting and Political Emotions." *Mobilization* 7, no. 2 (2002): 129-140.

Barber, Benjamin. *Strong Democracy.* Berkeley CA: University of California Press, 1984.

Barabas, Jason. "How Deliberation Affects Policy Opinions." *American Political Science Review* 98, no. 4 (2004): 687-701

Bartels, Larry M. "Uninformed Votes: Information Effects in Presidential Elections." *American Journal of Political Science* 40, no. 1 (1996): 194-230.

Bartels, Larry M. "Homer Gets a Tax Cut: Inequality and Public Policy in the American Mind." *Perspectives on Politics* 3, no. 1 (2005): 15-31.

Baum, Matthew, and Angela Jamison. "The Oprah Effect: How Soft News Helps Inattentive Citizens Vote Consistently." *Journal of Politics* 68, no. 3 (2006): 946-59.

Beck, Paul Allen, Russell J. Dalton, Steven Greene, and Robert Huckfeldt. "The Social Calculus of Voting: Interpersonal, Media, and Organizational Influences on Presidential Choices." *American Political Science Review* 96. no. 1 (2002): 57-73.

Bendor, Jonathan, Daniel Diermeier, Michael Ting. "A Behavioral Model of Turnout." *American Political Science Review* 97. no. 2 (2003): 261.

Benhabib, S. "Toward a Deliberative Model of Democratic Legitimacy." *In Democracy and Difference,* edited by S. Benhabib. Princeton NJ: Princeton University Press, 1996.

Bennett, Stephen E., Richard S. Flickinger, and Staci L. Rhine. "Political Talk Over Here, Over There, Over Time." *British Journal of Political Science* 30, no. 1 (2000): 99-120.

Bent, Flyvbjerg. "Ideal Theory, Real Rationality: Habermas Versus Foucault and Nietzsche." Paper presented at the Political Studies Association-UK 50th Annual Conference, London, April 10-13, 2000.

Berelson, Bernard R., Paul F. Lazarsfeld, and William N. McPhee. *Voting.* Chicago: University of Chicago Press, 1954.

Bohman, J. "The Coming of Age of Deliberative Democracy." *Journal of Political Philosophy* 6, no. 4 (1998): 400-25.

Brown, Jacqueline Johnson, and Peter H. Reingen. "Social Ties and Word-of-mouth Referral Behavior." *Journal of Consumer Research* 14, no. 4 (1987): 350-362.

Brown, R. Khari, and Ronald E. Brown. "Faith and Works: Church-Based Social Capital Resources and African American Political Activism." *Social Forces* 82, no. 2 (2003): 617-42.

Cohen, J. "Deliberation and Democratic Legitimacy." *In Deliberative Democracy*, edited by J. Bohman and W. Rehg, Cambridge MA: MIT Press, 1997.

Coleman, James. *Foundations of Social Theory*. Princeton, NJ: Princeton University Press, 1990.

Coleman, James S., Elihu Katz, and Herbert Menzel. "The Diffusion of Innovations Among Physicians." *Sociometry* 20, no. 4 (1957): 253-70.

Coleman, James Samuel. "Social Capital in the Creation of Human Capital." *American Journal of Sociology* 94 (supp.) (1988): S95-S120.

Colletti, L. *Karl Marx: Early Writings*. Harmondsworth: Penguin Press, 1975.

Conover, Pamela Johnston, Donald D. Searing, and Ivor M. Crewe. "The Deliberative Potential of Political Discussion." *British Journal of Political Science* 32, no. 1 (2002): 21-62.

Cooke, Maeve. 2000. "Five Arguments for Deliberative Democracy." *Political Studies* 48, no. 5 (2000): 947-69.

Cox, D. F. "The Audience as Communicators." In *Toward Scientific Marketing*, edited by S. A. Geyser, Chicago: American Marketing Association, 1963.

Dalton, Russell J. *Citizen Politics: Public Opinion and Political Parties in Advanced Industrial Democracies*, 3rd Edition. New York: Chatham House, 2002.

Delli Carpini, Michael X., and Scott Keeter. *What Americans Know about Politics and Why It Matters*. New Haven: Yale University Press, 1996.

Downs, Anthony. *An Economic Theory of Democracy*. New York: Harper, 1957.

Druckman, James N. "Political Preference Formation: Competition, Deliberation, and the (Ir)relevance of Framing Effects." *American Political Science Review* 98, no. 4 (2004): 671-86.

Edwards, Bob, and Michael W. Foley. "Much Ado about Social Capital." *Contemporary Sociology* 30, no. 3 (2001): 227-31.

Gastil, John, and James Dillard. "Increasing Political Sophistication Through Public Deliberation." *Political Communication* 16, no. 1 (1999): 3–23.

Grofman, Bernard N., Guillermo Owen, and Scott L. Feld. "Thirteen Theorems in Search of the Truth." *Theory and Decision* 15, no. 3 (1983): 261-78.

Grofman, Bernard. "Reflections on Public Choice." Paper presented to the Public Choice Society, February 12, 2003.

Habermas, Jürgen. *The Theory of Communicative Action*. Vol. 1. Boston: Beacon Press, 1984.

Habermas, Jürgen. *The Theory of Communicative Action*. Vol. 2. Boston: Beacon Press, 1987.

Heckelman, Jac C. 2000. "Revisiting the Relationship Between Secret Ballots and Turn-out." *American Politics Quarterly* 28, no. 2 (2000): 194-215.

Herr, Paul M., Frank R. Kardes, and John Kim. "Effects of Word-of-Mouth and Product-Attribute Information of Persuasion: An Accessibility-Diagnosticity Perspective." *Journal of Consumer Research* 17, no. 4 (1991): 454-63.

Hetherington, Marc J. "The Political Relevance of Political Trust." *American Political Science Review* 92, no. 4 (1998): 791-808.

Huckfeldt, Robert. "The Social Communication of Political Expertise." *American Journal of Political Science* 45, no. 2 (2001): 425-38.

Huckfeldt, Robert and John Sprague. *Citizens, Politics, and Social Communication: Information and Influence in an Election Campaign.* New York: Cambridge University Press, 1995.

Huckfeldt, Robert, Jeanette Morehouse Mendez, and Tracy Osborn. "Disagreement, Ambivalence, and Engagement: The Political Consequences of Heterogeneous Networks." *Political Psychology* 25, no. 1 (2004): 65-96.

Huckfeldt, Robert, John Sprague, and Jeffrey Levine. "The Dynamics of Collective Deliberation in the 1996 Election: Campaign Effects on Accessibility, Certainty, and Accuracy." *American Political Science Review* 94, no. 3 (2000): 641-51.

Huckfeldt, Robert, Ken'ichi Ikeda, and Franz Pappi. "Political Expertise, Interdependent Citizens, and the Value Added Problem in Democratic Politics." *Japanese Journal of Political Science* 1, no. 2 (2000): 171-95.

Huckfeldt, Robert, Ken'ichi Ikeda, and Franz Pappi. "Patterns of Disagreement in Democratic Politics: Comparing Germany, Japan, and the United States." *American Journal of Political Science* 49, no. 2 (2005): 497-514.

Huckfeldt, Robert, P. E. Johnson, and John D. Sprague. *Political Disagreement: The Survival of Diverse Opinions Within Communication Networks.* Cambridge, UK: Cambridge University Press, 2004.

Ikeda, Ken'ichi, and Robert Huckfeldt. 2001. "Political Communication and Disagreement among Citizens in Japan and the United States." *Political Behavior* 23, no. 1 (2001): 23-51.

Jackman, Robert W. and Miller, Ross A. "Social Capital and Politics." Annual Review of Political Science 1, no. 1 (1998): 47-73.

Jervis, Robert. "The Drunkard's Search." In *Explorations in Political Psychology,* edited by S. Iyengar and W. McGuire, 338-60. Durham, NC: Duke University Press, 1993.

Kahneman, Daniel, and Amos Tversky. "Prospect Theory: An Analysis of Decision Under Risk." *Econometrica* 47, no. 2 (1979): 263-92.

Katz, Elihu, and Paul Lazarsfeld. *Personal Influence.* New York: The Free Press, 1955.

King, Gary, James Honaker, Anne Joseph and Kenneth Scheve. "Analyzing Incomplete Political Science Data." *American Political Science Review* 95, no. 1 (2001): 49-69.

King, Gary, Michael Tomz, and Jason Wittenberg. "Making the Most of Statistical Analyses: Improving Interpretation and Presentation." *American Journal of Political Science* 44, no. 2 (2000): 347-61.

King, Gary. "Statistical Models for Political Science Event Counts: Bias in Conventional Procedures and Evidence for The Exponential Poisson Regression Model." *American Journal of Political Science* 32, no. 3 (1998): 838-63.

King, Gary, Michael Tomz, and Jason Wittenberg. "Making the Most of Statistical Analyses: Improving Interpretation and Presentation." *American Journal of Political Science* 44, no. 2 (2000): 347-61.

Lau, Geok Theng, and Sophia Ng. 2001. "Individual and Situational Factors Influencing Negative Word-of-Mouth Behaviour." *Canadian Journal of Administrative Sciences* 18, no. 3 (2001): 163-178.

Lau, Richard. "Models of Decision Making." In *Oxford Handbook of Political Psychology,* edited by David O. Sears, Leonie Huddy, Robert Jervis, 19-59. Oxford, UK: Oxford University Press, 2003.

Lau, Richard R., and David P. Redlawsk. "Voting Correctly." *American Political Science Review* 91, no. 3 (1997): 585-99.

Lau, Richard R., and David P. Redlawsk. *How Voters Decide: Information Processing in Election Campaigns.* Cambridge, UK: Cambridge University Press, 2006.

Lazarsfeld, Paul, Bernard Berelson, and Hazel Gaudet. *The People's Choice.* New York: Columbia Univ. Press, 1944.

Leib, Ethan J. *Deliberative Democracy in America: A Proposal for a Popular Branch of Government.* University Park: Pennsylvania State University Press, 2004.

Levine, Jeffrey. "Choosing Alone: The Social Network Basis of Modern Political Choice." In *The Social Logic Of Politics: Personal Networks As Contexts For Political Behavior*, editied by Alan S. Zuckerman, 132-51. Philadephia: Temple University Press, 2005.

Linimon, Amy, and Mark R Joslyn. "Trickle Up Political Socialization: The Impact of Kids Voting USA on Voter Turnout in Kansas." *State Politics & Policy Quarterly* 2, no. 1 (2002).

Long, J. Scott. "Regression Models for Categorical and Limited Dependent Variables." *Advanced Quantitative Techniques in the Social Sciences,* Volume 7. CA: Sage Publications, *1997.*

Macedo, Stephen. *Diversity and Distrust: Civic Education in a Multicultural Democracy.* Cambridge, MA: Harvard University Press, 2003.

Maddala, G. S. *Limited-Dependent and Qualitative Variables in Econometrics.* Cambridge, UK: Cambridge University Press, 1983.

McAdam, Doug, and Ronnelle Paulsen. "Specifying the Relationship between Social Ties and Activism." *American Journal of Sociology* 99, no. 3 (1993): 640-67.

McDonald, Michael P. "Up, Up and Away! Voter Participation in the 2004 Presidential Election." *The Forum,* no.2 (2004): 4.

Mendelberg, Tali. 2005. "Bringing the Group Back Into Political Psychology: Erik H. Erikson Early Career Award Address." *Political Psychology* 26, no. 4 (2005): 637-650.

Miller, Warren, and Shanks, J. Merrill. *The New American Voter.* Cambridge, MA: Harvard University Press, 1996.

Mutz, Diana C. "Cross-cutting Social Networks: Testing Democratic Theory in Practice." *American Political Science Review* 96, no. 1 (2002): 111-26.

Mutz, Diana C., Paul M. Sniderman, and Richard A. Brody. *Political Persuasion and Attitude Change.* Ann Arbor: Univ. of Michigan Press, 1996.

NES 2000. The National Election Studies, Center for Political Studies, University of Michigan. Electronic resources from the NES World Wide Web site (www.umich.edu/nes). Ann Arbor, MI: University of Michigan, Center for Political Studies [producer and distributor], 1995-2002.

Neuman, W. Russell. *The Paradox of Mass Politics.* Cambridge: Harvard University Press, 1986.

Newey, Whitney. "Simultaneous Estimation of Limited Dependent Variable Models with Endogenous Explanatory Variables." *Journal of Econometrics* 36, no. 3 (1987): 231-50.

Page, Benjamin I., and Robert Y. Shapiro. *The Rational Public: Fifty Years of Trends in American's Policy Preferences.* Chicago: University of Chicago Press, 1992.

Petty, Richard E., John T. Cacioppo, and David Schumann. "Central and Peripheral Routes to Advertising Effectiveness: The Moderating Role of Involvement." *Journal of Consumer Research* 10, no. 3 (1983): 135-46.

Piven, Francis Fox, and Richard Cloward. *Why Americans Still Don't Vote.* Boston: Beacon Press, 2001.

Polsby, Nelson. *Community Power and Political Theory.* New Haven: Yale University Press, 1963.

Popkin, Samuel. *The Reasoning Voter: Communication and Persuasion in Presidential Campaigns.* Chicago, IL: University of Chicago Press, 1991.

Price, Vincent, Joseph N. Cappella, and Lilach Nir. "Does Disagreement Contribute to More Deliberative Opinion?" *Political Communication* 19, no. 1 (2002): 95-112.

Putnam, Robert D., Leonardi, Robert, and Nanetti, Raeffaela Y. *Making Democracy Work.* Princeton, NJ: Princeton University Press, 1993.

Putnam, Robert D. *Bowling Alone.* New York: Simon & Schuster, 2000.

Putnam, Robert D. "Social Capital Measurement and Consequences." *Isuma* 2, no. 1 (2001): Spring.

Putnam, Robert D. and Feldstein, Lewis. *Better Together: Restoring the American Community.* New York: Simon & Schuster, 2003.

Rabinowitz, George, and Stuart Elaine Macdonald. "A Directional Theory of Issue Voting." *American Political Science Review* 83, no. 1 (1989): 93-121.

Rawls, John. "Kantian constructivism in moral theory." *Journal of Philosophy* LXXVII, no. 9 (1980): 517-72.

Rawls, John. *Political Liberalism.* New York: Columbia University Press, 1993.

Riker, William H. and Peter C. Ordeshook. "A Theory of the Calculus of Voting." *American Political Science Review* 62, no. 1 (1968): 25-42.

Robinson, John P., and Mark R. Levy. "Interpersonal Communication and News Comprehension." *Public Opinion Quarterly* 50, no. 2 (1986): 160-75.

Rogers, Everett M. *Diffusion of Innovations.* New York: Free Press, 1962.

Rogers, William. "Regression Standard Errors in Clustered Samples." *Stata Technical Bulletin* 13, no. 3 (1993): 19-23.

Rorty, Richard. "Idealizations, Foundations, and Social Practices." *In Democracy and Difference,* edited by S. Benhabib. Princeton NJ: Princeton University Press, 1996.

Rosenstone, Steven, and John Mark Hansen. *Mobilization, Participation and Democracy in America.* New York: Macmillan, 1993.

Rousseau, Jean-Jacques "The Social Contract." *In The Social Contract and Discourses,* edited by G. D. H. Cole. London: Dent, 1973.

Rousseau, Jean-Jacques, Locke, John, and Hume, David. *Social Contract.* New York: Oxford University Press, 1960.

Sekhon, Jasjeet. "The Varying Role of Voter Information across Democratic Societies." Technical Report, 2004.http://polmeth.wustl.edu/retrieve.php?id=39.

Shapiro, Ian. "Enough of Deliberation: Politics is About Interests and Power." In *Deliberative Politics: Essays on Democracy and Disagreement,* edited by Stephen Macedo, 28-38. Oxford, UK: Oxford University Press, 1999.

Sheth, Jagdish. "Word-of-mouth in Low-Risk Innovations." *Journal of Advertising Research* 11, no. 3 (1971): 15-18.

Silverman, George. "How to Harness the Awesome Power of Word of Mouth." *Direct Marketing* 60, no. 7 (1997): 32-38.

Skocpol, Theda. "Unravelling from Above." *American Prospect* 25 (1996): 20-5.

Skocpol, Theda, and Marshall Ganz. "A Nation of Organizers: The Institutional Origins of Civic Voluntarism in the United States." *American Political Science Review* 94, no. 3 (2000): 527-46.

Sniderman, Paul M., Richard A. Brody, and Philip E. Tetlock. *Reasoning and Choice: Explorations in Political Psychology.* Cambridge: Cambridge University Press, 1991.

Strauss, Leo. *The City and Man.* Chicago: Rand McNally, 1964.

Taber, Charles. "Information Processing and Public Opinion." In *Oxford Handbook of Political Psychology,* edited by David O. Sears, Leonie Huddy, and Robert Jervis, 433-76. Oxford, UK: Oxford Univresity Press, 2003.

Tetlock, Philip E. *Expert Political Judgment: How Good Is It? How Can We Know?* Princeton: Princeton University Press, 2005.

The National Election Studies, Center for Political Studies, University of Michigan. Electronic resources from the NES World Wide Web site (www.umich.edu/~nes). Ann Arbor, MI: University of Michigan, Center for Political Studies [producer and distributor], 1995-2002.

Thompson, Dennis F. "Election Time: Normative Implications of Temporal Properties of the Electoral Process in the United States." *American Political Science Review* 98, no. 1 (2004): 51-63.

Tomz, Michael, Jason Wittenberg, and Gary King. 2003. CLARIFY: Software for Interpreting and Presenting Statistical Results. Version 2.1. Stanford University, University of Wisconsin, and Harvard University. January 5th. Available at http://gking.harvard.edu/

Tversky, Amos, and Daniel Kahneman. "The Framing of Decisions and the Psychology of Choice." *Science* 211, (1981): 453-58.

Valelly, Richard M. "Public Policy for Reconnected Citizenship." In *Public Policy and Democracy,* edited by Steven Rathgeb Smith and Helen Ingram. Washington, DC: The Brookings Institution, 1993.

Venkatraman, Meera P. "Opinion Leaders, Adopters, and Communicative Adopters: A Role Analysis." *Psychology and Marketing* 6, no. 2 (1989): 51-68.

Verba, Sidney, and Nie, Norman. *Participation in America: Political Democracy and Social Equality.* New York: Harper and Row, 1972.

Verba, Sidney, and Nie, Norman, Kim, Jae-On. *Participation and Political Equality.* New York: Cambridge University Press, 1978.

Walsh, Katherine C. *Talking About Politics: Informal Groups and Social Identity in America.* Chicago: University of Chicago, 2004.

Whyte, W. H. Jr. "The Web of Word of Mouth." *Fortune* (November 1954): 140-43.

Wooldridge, Jeffrey M. *Econometric Analysis of Cross Section and Panel Data.* Cambridge, MA: MIT Press, 2002.

Yack, Bernard. *The Problems of a Political Animal: Community Justice, and Conflict in Aristotelian Political Thought.* South Bend, IN: University of Notre Dame Press, 1997.

Zaller, John. *The Nature and Origins of Mass Opinion.* Cambridge, UK: Cambridge University Press, 1992.

Zuckerman, Alan S. "Returning to The Social Logic of Politics." In *The Social Logic of Politics: Personal Networks as Contexts for Political Behavior,* edited by Alan S. Zuckerman, 3-20. Philadephia: Temple University Press, 2005.

Index

About the Author

Sean Richey is an Associate Professor in the Department of Political Science at Georgia State University. He teaches and researches political communication and political behavior, with a specialization in voting behavior, political discussion networks, social capital, and political participation. He was a Japan Society for the Promotion of Science Post-Doc at the University of Tokyo in 2004 to 2006. In 2013-2014, he will be a Fulbright Scholar in Japan in residence at the University of Tokyo. He lives in Roswell, Georgia, with his wife and three children.

www.ingramcontent.com/pod-product-compliance
Lightning Source LLC
Chambersburg PA
CBHW051253050326
40689CB00007B/1181